ANYTHING
for
ACCEPTANCE

_____

Dr. Murl Edward Gwynn

First printing July, 2001
Second printing November 2008
Third printing 2013

Published by MEG Enterprises Publications
PO Box 2165
Reidsville, GA 30453
(912) 557-6507
meg@kencable.net
www.murlgwynn.com

Unless otherwise identified, Scripture quotations are from the
King James Version of the Bible

Scripture quotations marked NIV are from the Holy Bible New
International Version, copyright © 1973, 1978, 1984 by
International Bible Society. Zondervan Publishing House. Used
by permission.

Printed in the U.S.A

International Standard Book Number: 0-9711766-0-4

Acknowledgements

I acknowledge the King of Kings, Lord of Lords and soon coming Judge of the whole earth.

I acknowledge that I can do nothing without God's direct intervention and support. He is my sustainer!

My wife and best friend, Ruth, who endured the years and hurt with a man who learned the hard way. If there is a story told in this book, it is the story of one who stayed, when running would have stopped the pain.

Dedicated to

Ruth

You are the epitome of your namesake in scripture.
To say I love you would never be enough.
Where would I be without you?

CONTENTS

Foreword

When I received the request to write the foreword for "Anything for Acceptance," I sat down at my desk, with the manuscript, to enjoy reading about someone I knew well. But before long, I realized that Murl, while revealing the truth about his past life, was introducing me to a man I had never known. In fact, the Murl that I have known for some 17 years is nothing like the Murl described in the first part of this book. 2 Corinthians 5:17

As I read page after page, I felt a warm, deep love and appreciation in my spirit for the saving and changing power of the blood of our Lord Jesus Christ. Jesus not only died for Murl, but while we were <u>still</u> <u>sinners,</u> Christ died for us. Romans 5:8. We were all included.

Yes, the Murl that I know has the fruit of a totally changed man. For in Christ he is a new man-not a repaired man. God doesn't just patch us up. In Christ, the believer becomes a new creation with a new nature, with new goals, new values and new motivations, etc.

In addition to pastoral ministry, Murl is also a very vital part of the ongoing operation of the Fellowship of Churches and Ministers, International. He is a member of the board of Presbyters and is presently serving as Secretary and Treasurer of the fellowship. I am thankful to have him on the team.

I have enjoyed ministering at Christian Life Fellowship Church where Murl serves as pastor, and my wife and I are blessed each time we visit in the Gwynn home. The spirit of love, joy and peace is certainly present in the church and in the family, including their children. There is no "hangover" from the past! There is no condemnation present to kill the joy and fellowship. It is fun to visit with them, and Ruth serves some very tasty meals.

Ruth displays a quiet and gentle spirit, but she is a woman who is very capable of making her own decisions. I am of the opinion that Ruth did not stay with the "Old" Murl during those difficult times because of his promises and persuasion. It is evident that she walked in the marvelous grace (favor) of God that enabled her to forgive her husband and reap the rewards of total commitment to God in her marriage vows.

If your marriage is in trouble, please read this book before you make a decision to divorce. Remember, God loves you too.

Ed Robbins
Co-Founder
Fellowship of Churches and Ministers,
International

Introduction

This book is about one life that struggled with the desire to be accepted. It is my life and why I had such a difficult time with a poor self-image and the loathing brought on by sin and its effects at an early age.

I have met many people who have a similar story. These people find it hard to believe that someone cares or even knows they exist. That belief came from some action, thought, or event that caused them to feel unworthy. It is a terrible feeling and one, which, if there is no release, can lead to terrible consequences or at least a miserable life.

In my own struggle to be accepted, I looked in all the wrong places. I pray, if you are like I was that you would read this book with hope, surrender, and openness to the Spirit of God.

I can assure you, there is an answer to your predicament and heart's cry. Don't let any day go by without seeking God's will and ways. He knows you live, what you need, and what you are going through. Turn to Him!

If you are married and think that the best thing for you to do is divorce your spouse, I ask you to reconsider. Maybe you believe that your spouse does not love you because of his/her actions toward you. You may have good reasons to "want out," but I know this, if you will give

God an opportunity to work in your marriage and on your spouse there can be redemption in your marriage. **If you read anything in this book, read the chapter on "Ruth."** She stayed when she could have left me...thank God she didn't!

Acceptance can only be found in Jesus.

Dr. Murl Edward Gwynn
PO Box 2165
Reidsville, GA 30453
meg@kencable.net

Chapter One

How It All Began

It was a time of innocence, a time of dreams, and a time of experimentation. The nation was learning of great new things, but also of social issues that touched each citizen in their own way. No one was immune to the transcendence of the moment and everyone would benefit from its growth.

Needless to say I was no different from anyone else, and would realize my share of what society had to offer and its direction. I would experiment, test, and partake of the times just as many others did. My life was touched and my inner person would suffer, and like many men, I would have to find my way.

The topic and subject matter of this book is not the most sought after teaching by the average Christian. After all, Christians have it all together, right? Well, anyway, we will proceed with caution, but with determination, to get to the heart of the matter and hopefully be better off for it.

If you are a male reading this, I hope you will find the answers to those questions that nag many a testosterone infected human. Yes, we often have questions about our drives, desires, and wants. I may not be able to answer all of those questions, but I will surely give you my story and what drove me on like a wild stallion without a bit and bridle.

I will be sixty three this year.[1] I have been married for over 40 years to Ruth Lorraine Olson Gwynn, a wonderful, forgiving woman, who doesn't have a vicious bone in her body. We have three children, two sons-in-law, one daughter-in-law, two grandsons, two cats, and one blind dog. Life is good right now; well, I'm not too sure about the blind dog, but it wasn't always so.

---

[1] I put my fingers to the keyboard to start this book on March 23rd, 2001. The year of the second printing of this book was 2009.

The place to start is at the beginning. I will not try to bore you with petty things, but I will need to give you the probable whys, wherefores, and what ifs. You see, these are important to us all. Not that my story is any more or less important than yours, but we all have a story. Since where I am going in my story was directly affected by why I did what I did and the influences that led me to those human actions, I must share them.

So, beginning at an early age is most important to my story. I was born in a little town in the Dakotas. Carrington was not a busy and complex world of excitement in the late 40's and 50's, but it was home. I loved its people, its places, and its palaces. No, we didn't have real palaces, but when you are young, palaces can be made of anything that gives glamour, glory, and goose bumps. Being young and impressionable, I could pitch a tent at anything that would titillate my desires and satisfy my fantasies. It was probably for those reasons that I went astray later on in life.

I was the youngest of nine, yes, I said nine boys. We had a baseball team, a virtual team of strong, viral and outspoken guys. The Gwynn and Sharbono[2] boys were healthy, happy and full of fun- loving play. There was no lack of excitement or problems in our house. You name it and we probably did, tried, tasted or drank it. We probably weren't afraid of anything but getting caught. It was just that type of life and lifestyle that would get me into moral trouble later.

I loved my dad and mom very much. We had great times. Dad wasn't much of a talker, but he was a good, quiet provider for the family. He loved Mom and showed it in his own way. Mom loved Dad and demonstrated it through the many children, meals, help and kisses that made him dance. She was great! They were a modest, sincere couple who loved their children and did everything possible to insure we had enough. Although they are with Jesus

---

[2] The Sharbono boys were the oldest of the boys. Mother was married and divorced.

now, I can still hear them kissing before they went to sleep. Good night, Mom! Good night, Dad! I love you!

Back to the boys. Being the guys we were, and the nature of the times, it was inevitable that I would be introduced to sex in my home. No, nothing weird happened to me by my dad, mother or brothers, but it happened like it probably did to thousands of young people throughout the USA. Many girls and boys have a similar story to mine. The intro to titillating pornographic pictures and macho stories abounded among us boys. Being an impressionable young boy opened up to me things that I should never have had to deal with until later. Nevertheless I did. I will never forget the first encounter.

The First Encounter

I was probably six, seven, or eight. It was a sunny bright day, the kind that only a Dakotan would know. Spring was fresh and blooming with the new growth, new vigor and new adventures just waiting for the curiosity of young Murl Gwynn. As usual, I was snooping around the house, trying to find new things in other people's drawers, boxes, and the like. What I found in one box among the military memorabilia of one brother would catch my attention and possess me for years. It changed me from an innocent adventurer to a victim of curiosity of the flesh and desires of the human nature. Oh, that I would have been caught right then and there!

I wasn't caught, but I was hooked. I looked at those pornographic pictures as often as I could. They became pleasurable to me. They taught me how to please self by gazing at the naked body of a woman. I wanted more!

Obtaining more of the pleasure that came from those pictures was not long in coming. Another brother soon provided other pictures from his secret stash. Unbeknown to him, I would go into his bedroom and dig out the object of my pleasure and rush into the bathroom to be alone with my fantasies. Gazing at the adult books made me excited, feel grown up and dark.

Yes, I felt dark. No, I didn't feel like I was in the dark, I felt like I was dark. I felt like something was out of order, that something had left me off-colored, missing and WRONG! But, I wanted more! You see, when things like that are opened to a young mind, ahead of the natural time and order for growth, it causes addiction at a high level. I opened the door for demons, secret desires, and strange wants.

I can't blame those brothers or my parents, although my parents should have been more diligent in our home as to the items being brought in. The blame lies with a society that did nothing to stop the promotion and sale of corruptible material, without the least thought of its effects. The blame lies with churches and pastors that did nothing to stop it. The blame lies in the heart of man so corrupted by self that it is too lazy to pull itself up out of the bondage of uncontrolled desire. That is why we needed a pure selfless lamb for our sacrifice. Thank you, Jesus!

You can imagine what happened next. I sought out more sexually explicit books, movies, and women. These things brought momentary satisfaction and much experimentation. I grew socially, physically, and mentally, but I didn't grow through my innocence like every child should. I was thrust into a world of unsatisfying desires of the flesh. Oh, don't get me wrong; I wasn't some strange and wild person with a tattoo on my head that said, "I want sex!" The tattoo was affixed to my soul.

Soul, you see, is where the battle of those kinds of desire and want are waged. If our soul is not fed with the proper food of love, acceptance, and forgiveness, we will do anything to get it. Since sex can give pleasure, it is only natural to constantly want more of it, because it also feeds our soulish desires. It was those areas of acceptance that I came to realize were some of the causes for the things I did.

Looking back over the years, I have recalled moments of desperation for affection and attention, and the crazy things I did to get it. Like the time when I was around ten years old, a bunch of us kids were playing in the front yard, you know, trying to outdo each other for the position of "big man." To the other kids it was no big deal if they won or lost, but to me it meant being accepted and loved by getting everyone's attention. I had to do something! My plan was hatched! I saw the cactus; it was perfect. I would bump into the other guy and act like this encounter's force propelled me backward into the cactus, needles and all. What I forgot to calculate into my equation was the never forgiving attitude of those sharp, buttocks-piercing points. Wow, I sure got everyone's attention. All eyes were on me as I screamed like a banshee; running around the yard, mind screaming for relief and the gentle soothing of a mother's love. Into the house I ran, crying, yelling and pleading for comfort and acceptance. I found the relief from the needles, but lost the accolade of my peers by being so stupid as to do such a thing. They saw through my ruse!

There were other moments of desperation that led to unfulfilled inner satisfaction and lacked true feelings of self-worth. Each of those moments only added to my loathing of self and made me dig even deeper into things that fed the flesh but never the spirit. Yes, people can come to a point in their lives that they don't see their self-worth as worth much. This may sound dramatic, but when a person has a low self-esteem many things in his/her life will follow suit. Like the ole adage "Garbage in, garbage out!" I was only putting garbage into my life and, therefore, could only put out garbage, or so that is what I thought of my life.

I barely graduated from high school and probably made it because many of the teachers liked me in spite of my grades. They just wanted to help me get through; it didn't matter that I could hardly read. This lack of reading skills affected me for years, until I met the one who created the voice box, gave the breath, and provided language. Through all this and because I didn't measure up, I sought things that would give me pleasure and fill the need of happiness; or so I thought.

College

It was 1965, graduation, entering college, and loneliness. If ever there was a sad moment, it was the day I set foot on the campus of Valley City State Teachers College[3] in Valley City, North Dakota. I don't mean it was a sad day because I got into college; that was a miracle at the time, and one that perplexed me. You see, when I say I could hardly read, I mean I could hardly read. When I took the entrance exam for college, I didn't

---

[3] Valley City State Teachers College is still there, but is now called Valley City State College.

think I had any chance of getting into college; I was dumb and knew it. When the results of the exam came back, and I had passed and been accepted, I just figured someone had made a mistake and I had pulled one over on the establishment.

The sad day remark comes because the college experience only added to my feelings of inadequacy. From the moment I set foot on that campus I knew I shouldn't be there. The dark cloud of loathing had set in "real good" and I would wallow in it. There was only one escape from those feelings, and it was the bottle. College to me meant parties, girls, and spending money I didn't have.

I would go to classes, sit through lectures, and try to take notes that I couldn't read later on and really didn't care about. Every day became a tired mess of deeper despair of deadly deception brought on by last night's bottle of courage. There had to be something better.

Being raised a Catholic; I thought that maybe the priest would have some answers. After classes one day, I went to the Catholic rectory and met the priest, who invited me to supper. We went to the local pizza parlor and had pizza and beer. You can imagine the discouragement I felt sitting there getting drunk with a "Spiritual advisor," who, as the evening progressed, told me about his lack. Man, did I feel low!

You would have thought that I would have given up by that time, but I didn't. College was fun. If I didn't have to study, which I didn't, I could still make the most of time away from home. My roommate Arlen and I had some great times making fun of the eggheads. We would pull pranks on anyone, any time, and anywhere. Our great delight was messing around with "Chief," a Native American Indian in our dorm. I would go into his room at night, just before he would get back from studying, drinking, or whatever. Under his bed I would hide until he was just about asleep, then I would reach my hand up and over his face, screaming all the while! You can imagine the response I got from his fright. It charged me and made us all laugh beyond control. After Chief would "come to," I would have to make sure I was nowhere to be found; Chief was big and didn't take kindly to my scaring him like that. It would be great if I could find Chief now. I would apologize and thank him for not killing me. Really, Chief was a great guy, gentle, friendly, and smart. I could have learned from his together attitude and acceptance of everyone.

When I would go home, it was to have Mom wash my clothes, steal candy from Dad's restaurant and money from the cash register. He knew what I was doing but never said a word, ever! It wasn't until years later that I told him what I had done. He looked at me and quietly said, "I knew you were!" That was all there was to it.

Being home gave me some peace because I was looked at as the only son who ever went to college. I was the

"Man"!   You see, with that type of mentality, home was giving me acceptance based upon what I had accomplished, although I was accomplishing nothing.

After two semesters at college and flunking every subject but one, I was called into the Dean's office. Dean Bruen was a tall, Abraham Lincoln type, but without the beard. He was a nice guy who said what he wanted to say matter-of-factly. Looking across the desk at the "Dean," I just knew he saw me for who I was and for what I was doing. Our conversation went like this... "Mr. Gwynn, you are not doing very well in my college."

"No, Dean Bruen, I am not."

"Mr. Gwynn, I have a suggestion for you."

"What is it Dean Bruen."

"I think you should leave my college and join the Army, Mr. Gwynn."

"That is a good idea, Dean Bruen, I think I will." I walked out of his office and by the week's end I had left college.

Mom and Dad were disappointed that I had left college, but didn't seem to take it too hard. After raising nine boys, there weren't too many things that really surprised them. I hung around the house for a few weeks and then went down to the local Draft Board and volunteered for the military draft. Within a month or so, I was on my way to Ft. Leonard Wood, Missouri, for basic training.

The Lessons

There are a number of lessons that can be drawn from this time of my life. First of all, my feelings of low self-worth started because I got hooked on pornography. I felt unworthy, dirty and low. That low self-worth led me to other activities of sins of the flesh, and the more I partook, the lower I felt. It was a viscous road that I could have gotten off of by an operation of my will. However, my will didn't have any example or truth that it could latch onto. If I would have been given a pure example and a holy alternative, maybe I would have taken a different route.

As I stated earlier, I do not blame my parents. They were living and walking in the light and life they had. However, parents must learn that they have to play an active role in the lives of their children. **Prov 22:5 Thorns [and] snares [are] in the way of the forward (contrary and disobedient): he that doth keep his soul shall be far from them. 6 Train up a child in the way he should go: and when he is old, he will not depart from it.**

I encourage parents to "know" what is coming into their homes. This is not as easy as I may make it sound, but it must be done. Your child's bedroom is your room, in your house, and under your spiritual covering. Yes, give them the privacy that a child should be given, but you are ultimately responsible for their upbringing and spiritual health. If you don't do it, who will?

The next lesson is this: parents make sure you lead by example. Don't tell them or live like "Do what I say and not as I do!" It won't work!"

The third lesson is this: if you have an addiction to pornography or find yourself wandering off to the weaknesses of the flesh in that area, there is a way out. The way out is to go in another direction. I know this sounds simplistic, but it is the only way. The new direction obviously is Jesus.

When you find yourself being pulled to porn, it is at that time that you must replace it with something else. Something else must be pure, right and as satisfying as sex, mentally. The only thing I know that can be as satisfying as sex mentally is God. No, God is not going to sexually satisfy you, but you can find great joy, peace and comfort in His presence. Therefore, get on your knees, pray and call out to God for help. If you really mean it, He will give you a way out of that immediate pull of sexual pleasure.

I can't emphasize enough what I am going to say next. You must share your addiction with someone you trust. You will not be free on your own. When you share your problem with someone, it helps to act as a mental and spiritual policeman for your mind and soul. It is a reminder and a bridge to give you an out toward freedom

Chapter Two

Military Service

Lessons of love

It was 1966 and Fort Leonard Wood (Little Korea), Missouri, was my new home for a while. I took Dean Bruen's advice and went into the Army. Military service was something I was familiar with, as all of my brothers served as soldiers, sailors, or airmen. We had a proud, immediate heritage of service to our country. So it was just about natural for me to do my part.

Coming to the realization of what the army was all about shook my world. They actually expected me to listen, follow, and obey. These things were somewhat foreign to me as I was used to doing my own thing. If I wanted to drink, party, and sleep, I did. The army wanted me to be trained, tried, and tested for future action. My Drill Sergeant was constantly on my case for not listening or for making fun of the present situation we were in. If Sergeant Fanger was up to the task, I was up to the antagonism ministry of mayhem among our platoon. I laughed, joked, and disobeyed at every corner. Sergeant Fanger screamed, threatened, and gave me as many push-ups as I could take because of my lack of discipline. After all, who did he think he was, trying to tell me what to do? I was somebody, and he didn't have the right. "Right," I was somebody, all right. I was somebody who didn't feel like he measured up. Those feelings of low self-worth were demons that dogged me every day and night and caused me to fight, argue, and seek out dark avenues of the flesh.

One night something happened to get my attention. Since we were housed in old World War Two barracks, each recruit had to take his duty on "Fire Watch." Fire Watch was keeping a look out during the night for fires that could happen because of the old coal fired furnaces. It was about three in the morning, my eyes were heavy, and my mind was screaming for relief and sleep. Thoughts of home, how I felt about myself, my life, and Dad seemed to capture my attention. Dad, where did that come from? I didn't have a problem with my dad; I loved him and thought he was a nice guy. Why would I be thinking about him with the emotional affection of a little boy? I can't explain it, but I found the nearest toilet stall and cried my eyes out thinking about my dad. There was something happening to me that only comes from the spiritual side of man but gives vent when triggered by deep emotions of longing for the past. You see, dads are the direct link and natural example of a loving God for His creation and children. Although I didn't know it at the time, God was using my dad's position as my father to call me to Himself. That encounter with God, by thoughts of my father, set within me a desire for something that would be satisfied later on in Korea.

Fort Leonard Wood was full of adventures and tested every fiber of a young man's psyche, emotions, and manhood. The training I received was no different from any others over the course of history at "Little Korea," but it was my history in 1966. I learned to march, salute, and be a soldier and eventually found what it was like to take orders without back talk. My constant thought became, "Maybe I could be a decent soldier and learn to like this stuff." I put myself into the whole Army thing. I made my mind up to give it a try.

Fort Bliss

My trying of the Army continued through my Advance Individual Training (AIT) at Fort Bliss, El Paso, Texas. This hot, dry piece of government property was the training school for the world's Armies, and their missile men from their perspective countries. I was to be 16H, or as it is called in the army lingo, a "Sixteen Hotel"! A 16H at that time was a "Plotter." A "Plotter" was an individual who tracked enemy aircraft by receiving information through a headset and then writing backward on a clear

Plexiglas board the coordinates of that plot. I liked being a "Plotter," as it gave vent to the artistic side of me. No, I couldn't draw on the plotting board, but it was challenging to my right brain thing.

We trained five days a week at Ft. Bliss and had every Saturday and Sunday off. I made the most of those weekends by going to Juarez, Mexico, just over the border. There were thousands of soldiers who did the same thing. We would go to the many bars and get drunk and spend money like we were making millions. By the second or third day after payday, we were broke, bummed out, and tired.

Juarez is where I would satisfy my sexual desires to the max. Every bar had back rooms for every kind of sexual act and contact that a person could want. If you had the money, there was nothing kept from you! Your every deep desire and need could be satisfied, or so I thought. My deep needs were never really satisfied, as sex never fed my spirit. Sex fed my flesh, but made me feel dirty, dark and alone again. It made me feel like I did when I was a young boy looking at my brother's dirty books and acting upon my fantasies with women.

I know these accounts of my sexual encounters are disturbing to the average reader, but this book is about just those things. It is important to come to an understanding of what causes many people to have the feelings of inadequacy like I had. I am convinced that the low self-worth thoughts of many people in society are caused by perverse sexual encounters early in life. When those encounters are never really addressed or dealt with, they lead to shameful feelings and manifested emotional outbursts.

Our training at Fort Bliss was exciting as it fed my desire for something new and different. We were being taught things that pulled on the adventurous side of a young man and caused me to recall many a war movie. I would be the hero who had the answers in a tough situation. My mind let me travel to the foreign places they were telling us about, places that many of us would be going to. Germany, Korea, and, of course, Vietnam were the main stay of deployment in those days. Vietnam did not sound too inviting to me, as a guy could get killed there. I may have been the hero in my dreams and mind, but I wasn't crazy! My feet never let my face take a beating, but I figured I wasn't fast enough to out run a Vietcong's bullet. No, thank you!

We would have night training in which we had to find our way from point to point using a compass. That was exhilarating, but just a little scary, as there were rattlesnakes in the desert where this training took place. Those venomous vipers with silent lips didn't care if you were a big tough soldier or not. In the dark of the night they would strike at anything that came too close for their safety. I made my mind up that I would be nice and friendly, quiet, and discreet in my movements, but carry the largest rock I could to kill the night visitors if I found one.

In spite of the long fanged friendlies, I loved being in the dark trying to find my way with that compass. Our destinations were about a mile apart and we were timed, so we had to make sure we didn't dawdle in our quest for completion, but there was enough time to enjoy the cool crisp air and the star lit sky. I loved it! Even though there might have been rattlers around, I would stop, lie down on my back and stare up into the sky and take in every twinkling piece of light that quietly blinked its message of its creator's praise. Even though I was lost as the day was long, I had a sense of God's presence in that dusty, tumbleweed garden of sand. I was amazed at the vastness of it all. "There must be a God," I thought. At that instant my mind went tilt and caught a fleeting moment of truth that made me stop dead in my life and say, "If there is a God, then I must give an account!"

Since time was getting short and I had to get to my next point on the compass course, I didn't inhabit those thoughts of God or my having to give an account. Wow, I was sure glad that I was in a hurry, because if I would have had more time, I probably would have come under great conviction. I knew what I was doing in my life, my lewd thoughts, my craving for the wrong things and the disregarding of God's commands.

Shipped out...Germany

After a few weeks of "leave" in Carrington, I was off to Germany and my new assignment. My excitement grew as the airplane touched down in the land of dark beer, lederhosen[4], and Hitler. What I was expecting to find in this land of clean highways, well-kept yards, and fast on-time trains, I didn't know. Our American movies have a tendency to form our thinking to the point of ridiculousness. Maybe I was looking for the sexually loose women I heard about from many of the older soldiers who had been stationed in Germany in times past. After being there awhile, I came to see the German women as proud, warm, and not as loose as I wanted. In any case, I was on a new adventure with self and service to Country.

Within a few days I was sent to Wassacupa, Germany, an area north east of Fulda. "The Wassacupa"[5] was the training site for Hitler's glider pilots during the Second World War. It had a commanding view of the surrounding hills and mountains and spoke of its beauty by

---

[4] Lederhosen is the German name for short legged pants worn by traditional German men.
[5] Wassacupa is the German word "water cup."

showing off its glamour to anyone who would stop to enjoy its rugged simplicity. On any given day, there were hundreds of Germans enjoying the slopes and fresh air. In the winter, as everything gave way to the dormancy of snow, you could ski for miles down the mountain to awaiting "guesthouses." I frequented the many guesthouses as often as possible; many a dark night we would ski through the woods and down the mountain to them. I found the beer, blonds, and buddies fed my soulish appetite for more of the darker side of my life.

Our purpose for being in that specific place in Germany was to watch for Russian aircraft that might attack from the east. The Army used the Air Force's radar to detect the many planes that might use the closeness of that region. By then I was a Specialist Fourth Class (SP4) and assigned to the radar site on the hill. We were to be the lookout eyes for our missile sites and warn them of aircraft attack. It was fun conducting drills that made the many Hawk Missile Batteries[6] go on alert and conduct mock missile firings.

My off duty time was taken up in the NCO Club or in the village. Liquor became my constant friend and needed reliever of "self." I hated myself and didn't care much about anything other than getting drunk or being with

---

[6] An emplacement for one or more pieces of artillery.

prostitutes or unsuspecting German girls. I would take my weekend passes or special off time and go to Frankfurt to spend the entire time drinking and frequenting the many places of ill repute. These things gave momentary relief from the sense of "lost something" in my life that I couldn't quite get a handle on.

There were good things about being a soldier in Germany as well. Meeting guys from all over the USA and learning about their homes and backgrounds fed my curiosity for new things. Making friends in the military comes easy, as everyone is in the same boat, in a manner of speaking. You have the same lingo (Military terms), live in the same type of housing, eat the same food, and obviously wear the same clothes. When you met someone you felt comfortable with, you would share your stories, do the same things, and plan your next adventure or quest together.

One of my buddies was Jerry Brunette. Jerry was an Air Force policeman. He had a wonderful personality, but seemed to me to be out of place as a cop. He would tell me stories about what he wanted to be when he got out of the military. He wanted to be and did become an Undertaker! An Undertaker? Go figure! His dead body contact desire never ceased to amaze me. At least, that is what I thought his occupation would be. This was the guy we would get drunk with and then lead him to the attic and turn off the lights when he was not looking. He would stand petrified, screaming at the top of his lungs because he was afraid of the dark. Sure, becoming an Undertaker, in a room with a dead person, how could he do it? But do it he did!

Jerry accepted me the way I was and the things I did. He and his wife Shirley befriended me, welcomed me, and shared my life while in Germany. We spent many hours together on camp outs, going on tours, and some church things. They both were church-going people, and since they were Catholic too I would go with them when I had promised to and couldn't get out of it. God didn't mean much to me, but religion has a way of pulling you in, which is what happened to me.

I started to go to Sunday Mass[7] and became friends with the priest. He was a very nice guy and took time with me. We would sit for hours and talk about life, and the military, but very little about God. Our discussions were religious in nature and involved how to help people. Jesus, God and the like had nothing much to do with it. It was just about being good and helpful. I would try anything to be good, even if it meant religion. Don't forget, my life was a mess, and being good was something I knew I wasn't.

---

[7] Mass is what Catholics call their service.

One time I went on a "Religious Retreat" with the Catholic men of the unit. Our destination was to be France and some of the sites where "The Virgin Mary"[8] was supposed to have revealed herself to children. I really didn't care about the sites or "Mary" per se, but going to France was exciting. We would see the sites during the day and at night indulge ourselves in the local wine, women, and dance. Don't get me wrong; many of the people on the tours did not do the darker side of France, just those like myself who could care less. Even the priest would come with us and get drunk. With that type of example, it was a wonder I even contemplated becoming a Catholic Brother[9]. Please understand, I don't and didn't think all priests were like the ones I had met so far in my life. There are many God fearing lovers of Jesus who have given their lives in celibacy to the cause of Christ and do not partake of the things of darkness.

Go Home Boy

---

[8] "Virgin Mary" is the term used by Catholics to depict Mary the mother of Jesus. However, Mary had other children after Jesus' birth. See Luke 2:7 "And she brought forth her firstborn son, and wrapped him in swaddling clothes, and laid him in a manger; because there was no room for them in the inn."

[9] A Catholic Brother is like a priest, but without taking the vows of celibacy.

My two years in Germany quickly came to an end, and it was time for me to make up my mind...either re-enlist or get out and go home. Although I didn't know what I would do if I got out, I chose to throw in my green towel, stop polishing my boots, and go back to the "world"[10] and civilian life.

We all cheered as the airplane landed in New Jersey after our eight-hour flight from Rein Main, Germany. Fort Dix was the "out processing" center at that time and received us unruly troops with a smile and tactical tolerance. In just a few hours we were "out of there" and on other flights to our homes. I must admit, there was a little twinge of remorse as I boarded the plane and knew that I had just burned a bridge from the past. What lay ahead of me was scary and un-nerving because I had no prospects for a job or place to live.

Fargo, North Dakota, greeted me with a warm sunny day, gentle breezes, and the thoughts of "Here we go!"

The Lesson

Our lesson in this chapter is for fathers. I loved my father and never had a problem with him. He was a nice guy, but he didn't know how to give love in return. He was from the old

---

[10] The "World" is the USA for any soldier who is away from it.

school of thought that believed being strong and quiet were good examples of being a man. His lack of showing love to his sons affected some of them for life. I think some of the approval I was looking for was that which I didn't get from Dad. Dad never said, "I love you!" without first hearing it from others.

Fathers, show and speak love to your children! Don't let them think you love them; tell them so! **Prov 27:5 (NIV) Better is open rebuke than hidden love.**

Chapter Three

Fargo- New Things

Fargo, North Dakota, was one place that had special memories for me. It was the place that my high school girl friend was going to college (NDSU). Oh, yes, I had a girlfriend! I didn't mention it earlier, as I did not want to mention her name, nor the names of too many other people in my story. Suffice it to say that we dated for about two years before I went into the Army, and I saw her when I came home on a thirty day leave from Germany. She was a very nice person and fun to be around. Her ambitions in life were probably a little different than mine, and for that reason we broke up after I got back.

I can remember the day we broke up. I had just gotten a job at Welu Dental Laboratories in Fargo and went to see her. We went to my apartment, as I wanted to show her my new place. We sat and talked about the future, jobs, her schooling and us. Being the crazed guy I was, I just wanted to have sex with her, but instead of exploring that desire, I had the thought of just asking her if I could kiss her. Now, I'm sure you know by now that this was a little out of the ordinary for me, but for some strange reason I felt like just asking her for the kiss. This kiss would have been the first after I got back from Germany, as I didn't have time to stop before going to Carrington. She looked surprised and said, "You don't have to ask to kiss me." I kissed her and knew that we did not have a future together. We talked some more and after a short while I took her back to the college. That was the last time I saw her for a long time.

Why do I share about this? Well, I think it is to let you know that there are forces outside of ourselves that pull on our heart strings at moments that can make or break our futures. That moment with her was, I think, one of those times. I now believe that God was at work, wooing and calling me even though I didn't know Him.

The Lab

By the time I got out of the Army I could comprehend and retain grammar and English a little better (this is not saying much, however) and had enough confidence to find a job. I had a friend, Diane Kosey, who worked as a Dental Technician at Welu Dental Laboratories in Fargo. She told me to come to the "Lab" and apply for a job. I told her I didn't know anything about dentistry. She stated that Mr. Welu would hire people if they did well on the test he gave them. Test! My mind went nuts! Here we go again with the reading, studying and grades. No, Diane informed me, it was not that type of test, but just to test your dexterity. I took the test, passed and was hired.

I walked through the "Lab" in my new sharkskin suit, trying to look important as Mr. Welu showed me around after the test. People looked, wondering who this handsome man was. Was he a doctor, dentist, an important client of Mr. Welu's, or some other great friend of his? Who was he? Yeah, you got it right, those were my thoughts, I still had a problem with self-worth. It was thoughts like that that gave me self-approval because I thought no one else would.

The "Lab" was exciting for a while. I became the guy who poured concrete type material over handcrafted carvings of the human dental structure. These castings, as they were called, were then heated to thousands of degrees until the wax forms that were encased melted away. This left a hollow for hot metal to be centrifugally forced into. It wasn't hard work and soon became very boring. I wouldn't last long at this job.

My time out of the Army wasn't much different than when I was in, as far as the drinking and women went. I continued to feed my flesh and lose myself in the bottle. I dated some, but soon found that most of the women never enjoyed drinking like I did, so I partied, played, and went my own way for a while.

Who is that girl?

The one bright thing that happened at the "Lab" was Ruth. She caught my eye almost from the very first day, even though she wasn't throwing out a hook. I kept looking at this quiet, very attractive girl who kept pretty much to herself and didn't bother anyone. She worked in the "bite block"[11] department and did her job with efficiency and accuracy, as far as I knew.

Diane saw me looking at Ruth. "Who is that girl?" I said.

"That's Ruth Olson!"

"I'm going to get a date with her!"

"She's informally engaged," stated Diane.

"I don't care, I will get a date" I said. And for the following weeks I did everything I could to get a date with her. I would follow her across the street to the little grocery store at lunchtime. As we passed I would ask her for a date and she would refuse. I kept this up for weeks until one day she said yes. You see, she was mad at her

---

[11] The "bite block" is the item that a dentist uses to make an impression of the patient's teeth.

boyfriend and went out with me to get even with him. I didn't know about her and the boyfriend, and wouldn't have cared. All I knew was that that pretty girl would date me.

Our first date was a typical Murl function. I was broke because I had been drinking up all my money, so Ruth had to pay for our first date. Looking back over it now, she probably would have stayed away from me if she had known what was in store for her in the future. Nevertheless, she and I became an "item" and I considered her my "girl." I proposed marriage to her the first week I knew her. We were married six months later on October 12th, 1968. I like to say "I chased her until she caught me!"

From Job to Job

Our marriage was okay, but would not have been written up in any bridal magazine as the way to do it. We went to work, came home, went to work, and came home. Working at the same place was not conducive to a flowing relationship, as we had nothing to talk about that was different. I didn't like the "Lab" any more and could not put up with some of the other workers. Actually, my bad temper would get the best of me, and I would blow up at people easily. I had to try something else.

Our landlord had his own insurance business and accepted me into the firm. Amazingly, I studied for the State Insurance License examination and passed. Even though that test was hard and I barely made the grade, I had my license to sell life insurance. You would think I would have come to a better understanding of my self-worth and my abilities, but I didn't. I didn't see the passing of that test as any great success; I just figured someone messed up again. When you are down on yourself, there isn't much that can change the dogged loathing of self.

I was a terrible insurance agent. I sold very few policies and was not making enough to cover the "Income Loan" that my boss set up to live on. I didn't know it right away, but my employer fixed it with the bank to pay me a monthly income, but it was a loan and not a salary. Because the policies were not bringing in enough income to off set the loan, I was going in debt fast. When I realized what was going on, I refused the loan and quit. The motto of the insurance business I worked for was "Ya gotta wanna!" He meant, "You got to want to buy insurance before you will buy insurance!" I came to see it as "He wanted to take people for all they were worth," and I quit.

Ruth was concerned and upset because I quit the "Lab" and now the insurance business, but didn't fight with me too much. She just wanted me to find something and be happy. Happy I wasn't. I felt very insecure because of my failures and shortcomings. I drank a lot and my temper would get the best of me. Usually Ruth would be on the receiving end of my outbursts.

After a few weeks of looking for work, I became desperate. One day while looking at the want ads, I read the following employment opportunity: "Wanted, Experienced welder and mechanic. Apply at American Wheel and Brake." I knew I had to get something so Ruth would be happy with me, so I went and applied for the job.

American Wheel and Brake (AWB) was a company that made, repaired and maintained "Tractor and Trailers." You know, the eighteen-wheel kind. Orville, the Foreman, knew his business and was looking for experienced men to help maintain and repair the many rigs that came to AWB for expert care. He sat down behind his desk and started to ask me questions about my qualifications. "How many years experience as a mechanic?"

Looking sheepishly at him, I said, "None!"

"How many years experience as a welder?"

"None!"

"Why in the world did you come here to apply then?"

"Because I need a job, real bad!" I stood to my feet, pointed my finger at Orville and said, "But, sir, if you will train me, I will be the best welder and mechanic you have!"

Orville looked amazed and impressed, stating, "If you have enough guts to come here with that reason, you got the job!"

Wow! I got the job! Now I had to live up to those big mouth words. Had my bravado gotten me into trouble again? I worked very hard to learn every task required of me. Orville taught me personally and I became the only man, other than Orville, who did aluminum welding at AWB. I would crawl inside gas tankers, ignoring the dangers of insufficient steam timing, and weld away. Orville would get on my case time after time for not being safe enough. I would ignore Orville and keep on doing other unsafe practices. My temper soon got the best of me and I was fired, or as I like to say, "I quit a second before he fired me!"

Getting fired from the AWB job was probably inevitable as I was always tired, upset and with a hangover. I would leave work around 4:30PM each day and slowly make my way home stopping at the many bars that lined the traffic route from work. When I would get home, I would be moderately drunk and in no mood to answer to Ruth. Being tired because I didn't get enough sleep made me irritable at work and failing in my work safety and output. Getting fired was the right thing for Orville to do to a guy like me.

After AWB, I found a job as a "Sand Blaster" at Stagger Manufacturing. I would dress up in a protective suit and sand blast the by-products of welding off of tractor frames. That job was a very unattractive, everyday deadening of the senses. I hated it with a passion! If only I were a better person!

Shenanigans

Ruth's response to all of my actions was what you would expect; she was mad, frustrated, and very disappointed in me. I knew her thoughts as I could see her disdain for me in her eyes. This did nothing for my self-esteem, but who could blame Ruth? She had every right to be mad. If I would have been on the receiving end of my shenanigans I don't know what I would have done in her place. I knew she was praying for me to change, but, boy, did she have her job cut out for her.

Since we were married in the Lutheran Church, she wanted me to go to church with her. We found a nice Lutheran church not too far from our house and started to attend. I took instruction classes to become a member. I would sit through the sermons and come under conviction but do nothing about it. Ruth lived what she was taught and made me feel like a dope. I loved her, in my own way, but just couldn't measure up. Married life to me caused me to be more insecure because I knew I was not the man to my wife that I should be.

Sundays to me were just a day off from work. Ruth would get up and prepare to go to church and I would stay in bed. She always asked, "Are you going to Church with me?" I would repeat the same old thing, "No!" She would return from church and make my dinner and act like nothing had happened. What a woman!

When Ruth's relatives would come to visit; I would get up in the middle of conversations and tramp off to bed, leaving everyone just sitting there. Ruth would continue the conversations, trying to act like she was handling it, but I now know, she was dying on the inside. I was self-centered and self-absorbed.

Ruth lived through my frustration and constant belittling of her, which came from my own insecurities. I often wondered why she didn't just leave me. Her own frustrations had to be deep. There were moments that she gave vent to those frustrations, however. She told me the following story years later.

One night just after we came home from an evening out at the Lab's Christmas party, Ruth, who had walking pneumonia, released some of her frustrations and tension on me. We, or should I say, I had been drinking heavily. We had been arguing over something or the other, as I always found a way to be offended. Entering the house I kept up the bantering and trying to make a point, but I was too far-gone to make sense or to keep my wits about me. I guess (I can't remember the rest) I was in the middle of a sentence and passed out on the floor. Ruth was amazed and surprised and thought I was not breathing. She got down on the floor beside me, listened to my heart to see if it was beating, then got a mirror and put it under my nose to see if I was breathing. Realizing that I was breathing and not dead, she got mad! Mad she was and that madness got vented through her feet. You see, she stood to her feet and kicked me in the ribs one good solid kick. She was so mad and frustrated with her obnoxious, drunk, self-centered husband.

I did not wake up through the kick of my precious bride. In the morning, I couldn't understand why I felt so terrible. I had been drunk before, but this hangover was the worst ever. I couldn't understand why my ribs hurt so much. Ruth didn't say anything and gave no explanation to the night's activities. As far as I know, she never did anything like that again. However, I did, and would get drunk many times after that.

The Lessons

Our first lesson in this chapter is this: If you are struggling with a bad temper, a short fuse, or a chip on your shoulder, share your heart with someone. If you are married, share your feelings with your spouse. Just by telling them that you hurt, you can find relief. Maybe you would not get the total desired freedom you are looking for, but it will be a release and an open door for God to plant truth. Yes, you have to make yourself vulnerable, but it will be a step in the right direction. **Jame 5:16 Confess [your] faults one to another, and pray one for another, that ye may be healed. The effectual fervent prayer of a righteous man availeth much.**

The second lesson: Stop and look at yourself, no, not at all the bad that you put on yourself, but look at your total being. You have talents, gifts, and abilities that you may not recognize right now because of your immediate problems. Nevertheless, they are there. Believe me! If I had realized my abilities, maybe I would have made other choices. Every person is made unique and with God given talents. Let God show you yours! **Psal 139:13 (NIV) For you created my inmost being; you knit me together in my mother's womb. 14 I praise you because I am fearfully and wonderfully made; your works are wonderful, I know that full well. 15 My frame was not hidden from you when I was made in the secret place. When I was woven together in the depths of the earth,**

Chapter Four

Army Again

Our marriage and my work were going nowhere. We had happy moments, obviously, but for the most part it was a daily endurance test for Ruth. My job was a constant point of let down for me, and I wanted more. I was very unhappy, to say the least. One day Ruth said, "Why don't you reenlist in the Army? You always talked about it like you liked it." It sounded like a good idea, so I went down to the recruiter's office and applied. The Army welcomed me back with open arms. I got my rank back, did not have to redo Basic Training, and gained two years for pay. That was a pretty good deal; we were young so we gave it a try. The year was 1970.

After a few weeks in Seattle, undergoing a physical, getting new uniforms, and receiving orders, we were off to Selfridge Air Force Base in Mount Clemens, Michigan. I was to be an Operations Specialist in the S2[12]. This job was

---

[12] S2 is the staff office that handles classified material and Army security.

challenging and made me think. I still felt insecure, but I was earning a reputation for being a top-notch soldier, and one who was very capable of getting the job done. In a very short time I was made the clerk of all classified documents at the Headquarters. My duties brought me into contact with high-ranking officers who trusted me and made me feel proud. For a short time in my life, there, I could cope.

Dana

Ruth and I were getting along much better, as I curtailed my drinking. We saw the sights of Detroit and visited friends we knew there and had our first child. Dana was born on March 5th, 1971. Weighing in at a whopping 4 pounds, 13 ounces, she had to stay in the hospital for two weeks, as she had yellow jaundice from being two weeks premature. We were proud parents and loved to take many pictures of precious Dana. Dana is married now with two boys, Franklin and Nash.

Dana had it rough, being the first-born and growing up with a father who had a bad temper, drank too much, and looked for perfection that he himself did not have. Although she is a bright, well-adjusted woman now, she has had to work through areas of her life that were affected by me.

Many children have had their lives adversely affected by parents who took their shortcomings out on their children or spouses. Because I was struggling with my own personality and low self-worth, I projected those feelings onto Dana. That type of projection is a story told by many adults who later on in life have had to come to grips with love, acceptance and forgiveness.

If you are one of those who were adversely affected by a parent, let me assure you there is always hope. Jesus is the one you run to and receive acceptance from. He knows who you are and the great worth you are to God. Don't let feelings of low self-esteem rob you of your gifts and talents. You have much going for you, and Jesus can bring everything to a bright realization. Turn the past into a learning experience that others can benefit from. Look to Jesus, rest in the love God and your parents have in you now. You are worth much, capable of great things, and your future is controlled by Jesus.

Having a child made me more responsible and caused me to think of God more often, but I still had a long way to go to meet Him. We began to go to the Military Chapel and settled into our new life as a "Military Family."

San Francisco

After a year at Selfridge I received orders for a new assignment at the Presidio in San Francisco. California was the place of sun, fun, and living in sub-standard quarters. I was assigned to Mt. Tamalpias and a radar site that would observe the west coast for missile and aircraft attacks. The forty-five minute drive up and down the mountain each day was interesting.

That drive took me past areas that would pull on my sexual desires and cause me to go astray again. There were nude beaches, loose women, and hitchhikers who always had drugs. I never took the drugs but would try the beaches and the women.

The quarters or the military housing we were in was old, to say the least. The Army didn't charge us our whole housing allowance because they were so old and needed repair badly. Old Fort Baker was to be our home for one year. During that time I made the grass grow when everybody told me it was no use. We fixed up that house to our satisfaction and waited for our name to come to the top of the waiting list for new quarters. We came to the number one position the week we left for my next assignment.

We left San Francisco in December of 1971. I was going to Korea and Ruth would be living with her parents in Oriska, North Dakota. I didn't know it at the time, but Korea would be the place that ole Murl Gwynn would come to the end of his sexual rope, find true acceptance, and die.

The Lessons

Our lesson in this chapter revolves around God's sovereign plan. God is always at work, guiding, setting up and directing situations. He "always" responds to prayer and an honest heart. Being in the Army I know now was God's sovereign plan for my life. Being saved and becoming a pastor, obviously, was God's plan. To get me into the Army God had to guide.

When I was about eleven, I witnessed one of my brothers and my parents arguing. My brother was drunk and out of control. He was hollering at Dad and threw back his fist like he was going to strike out at him. As his fist went back, it hit and broke the door window. It startled my parents, and my brother and scared me. My mother became hysterical and ran to her bedroom crying. She stayed there, emotionally drained for days. I thought she was dying.

During Mom's time in bed, I knelt by my bed every day and prayed to God. I told Him that if He would help Mom, I would one day serve Him. I meant it with my whole heart. God meant it too, but He had to get me into a place and a situation that would bring about His will. The Army was the plan and situation. He is always at work for our good and His will. **Romans 8:28 And we know that all things work together for good to them that love God, to them who are the called according to [his] purpose. 29 For whom he did foreknow, he also did predestinate [to be] conformed to the image of his Son, that he might be the firstborn among many brethren. 30 Moreover whom he did predestinate, them he also called: and whom he called, them he also justified: and whom he justified, them he also glorified.**

Another time, this is after I was saved, I was feeling low and wondering where God was. He told me, "I have always been directing you. Even when you didn't know me, I was there. Do you remember working on Anwhiler's farm as a young man?" I did remember and this is what He told me. "The day you were cutting grass and just about lost your foot by the mower's blade, I was there! I protected your foot so that you could go into the Army and meet Jack and Bill! I have always been there watching over you, you were to become one of mine."

The mower incident:

It was a warm summer day and Mr. Anwhiler asked me to cut the grass. The front yard was small so I used the push mower instead of the riding mower. I would push and pull the mower as needed around trees and shrubs. The Anwhiler's had many chickens and sometimes the feathers would be over the yard. This particular day as I was cutting the grass, pushing and pulling, I noticed what I thought was a white feather on my shoe. I kicked my foot trying to dislodge the feather from my shoe, without any success. It became so annoying that I finally stopped the mower and looked down at my shoe. What I saw made me sweat. I had pulled the mower over my foot and the top part of my shoe was gone. The mower blade was below the area of the cut on my shoe, which meant that for some "freaky" reason I didn't lose my foot. I really felt "lucky" that I didn't get hurt. God however, was there protecting me! **Jere 29:11 (NIV) For I know the plans I have for you," declares the LORD, "plans to prosper you and not to harm you, plans to give you hope and a future. 12 Then you will call upon me and come and pray to me, and I will listen to you. 13 You will seek me and find me when you seek me with all your heart.**

Chapter Five

Korea

After a thirty-day leave in North Dakota, visiting our parents, making arrangements for Ruth to live with her parents, and insuring that our VW bus was in proper working order for Ruth, I was off to Ft. Lewis, Washington, for orders and transportation to Korea.

Ft. Lewis was not an exciting place as it was just a stopover for the many thousands of soldiers who were departing for the Orient. These soldiers didn't care much about "The Lewis" and did everything possible to be away from the place until departure time. As soon as we would find our barracks, meet one another and make friends, we were off to the bars and nightspots of Tacoma, Washington. It didn't matter how long we were going to be there, we were off for "fun."

Fun was a relative word to me then, as most of my actions were dictated by my feelings of low self-worth. I just wanted to be accepted! I know what you are thinking: if I wanted to be accepted, why didn't I act different? Well, the only way you can answer that is to have a proper mental attitude about yourself. Usually, people who are looking for attention, acceptance, and proper self-worth do just the opposite to get it. Then when they get close to receiving it, they run because it is not natural to them. What a mess we can get into when things get out of order early in life.

Fun at Ft. Lewis meant getting drunk, spending the night with girls we found at the bars and feeling terrible the next day. It didn't matter to me that Ruth was being the good Christian person she was supposed to be. It only mattered to me to lose myself in drink and sex. Yes, I cared for Ruth and would like to say I loved her, but true love would have never done any of those things[13]. I hated myself for going out on her, but by then I was too far-gone to give it much thought in the positive.

---

[13] 1Cor 13:4 (NIV) Love is patient, love is kind. It does not envy, it does not boast, it is not proud. 5 It is not rude, it is not self-seeking, it is not easily angered, it keeps no record of wrongs. 6 Love does not delight in evil but rejoices with the truth. 7 It always protects, always trusts, always hopes, always perseveres. 8 Love never fails..."

The Land of Kimshee

Korea was completely different from any place I had ever been. The land of mountains, rice paddies, and kimchee had a captivating allure to it that said "adventure" to me. As soon as we were off the airplane, we could smell an odor about the country. Everyone noticed it! What was it? I soon found out that the odor was kimchee, a fermented cabbage that every Korean ate. To my North Dakota nose, it smelled rotten and sickening. It was probably the best bug repellent you could get. I came to put up with the kimchee and learned to accept it as the norm.

Obviously, there was more to Korea than kimchee and the smells. Korea is a beautiful country, made up of proud people who have had more than their share of troubles. Korea's traditions go back thousands of years into the past and help form a people who want to be left alone to conduct their customs and direct their lives without fear of reprisals from foreign intervention.

The United States' presence in Korea was at their request to help defend against North Korea's attacks over the years. There were thousands of soldiers, airmen, and Marines in Korea, stationed in every nook and cranny of that beautiful country. I was one of many stationed at Osan Air Force Base, Osan, Korea.

Osan Air Base, being an Air Force installation, was more modern than most Army posts. We lived in modern billets that had all of the amenities that you could want. I lived in a private room, as my rank and position afforded me that luxury, but most guys had to live in a two man cubical with a curtain for the door. I was "lucky" to not have to put up with the noise, nonsense, and nocturnal activities of the average G.I.s[14] in a barracks setting.

I soon made friends with just about everyone in our unit and had no problem having companionship when off duty. One friend, Mike Huttner, a Chaplain's assistant and I were close, boozing buddies for years. Mike still laughs about our meeting in 1971.

Mike and Stew, new soldiers, had just come to our unit and were bunking in the same cubical. For some reason I got the idea that Mike and this other guy were trying to get a private room ahead of other people who had been there for some time. Since I was in charge of assigning rooms, I was not about to let these "newbies"[15] get a room before the others.

I went tramping down to Mike's cubical, barged in on them, and blurted out, "I don't care who you guys are, you are not getting a room ahead of the other guys." They looked shocked,

---

[14] G.I. is the acronym for Government Issue.
[15] Newbies is the term used to label new soldiers in a unit.

surprised, and confused! I turned around and tramped back to my room. That was that, I had told them! Mike, being the fun-loving guy he was, although he didn't like it, shook his head and laughed. He had just met Specialist Fifth Class Murl Gwynn. What a treat!

Being the guy I was, it didn't matter to me that I had just made a very bad impression on the new guys, I had made my point! In a very short time I was borrowing money from Mike for booze, prostitutes, and anything else I needed money for. We spent a lot of time together, laughing our way through Korea at anything and anyone who did not measure up to our standards. Mike's standards were better than mine, however, but that didn't matter to me, as I liked him tremendously. We are still friends today, and I even had the opportunity of leading him to Christ years later.

The Officers That Glowed

My duty assignment was in the office for operations. "Operations" was a section within the S3[16] that controlled the Hawk Missile Batteries in Korea. We insured that the missile sites were maintained, staffed, and functioning according to the plans and orders set down for

---

[16] S3 is the office for Plans and Operations in any Army Command.

them. I was the only NCO[17] in the office at that time. There was a Major, a Lieutenant, and two Captains in adjacent offices, who became the most important people in my life.

Those two captains claimed to be Christian, but sure acted different from any other Christians I had seen or heard before. Other than Ruth, I didn't know that there were Christians who lived what they were taught and believed the Bible. These guys seemed to have it all together. They didn't drink alcohol or go to the village like the rest of us did. They went to church (chapel), spent their time doing wholesome activities either at the craft shop or on tours, seeing the many sights of Korea.

Although I know better now, when I was around Captain Jack Lloyd and Captain Bill Law, they seemed to glow. Yes, I mean glow! They talked and lived Jesus! It was weird, observing those guys as they went about their daily activities and GLOWED. I didn't understand it, what did those guys have? Maybe I was losing my mind. After all, nobody else seemed to notice the glow.

I would lie to the Major just to be around the Captains. My desk was full of paper clips from telling my boss that we were out and I needed to go get some from the Captains. Jack and Bill knew that something was going on when I would

---

[17] NCO is the acronym for Non-commissioned Officer

show up at their office and stand, leaning on the doorframe, staring at them. The glow seemed to mesmerize me and I just had to have more of it. What I didn't know at the time was that God was fixin (as they say in Georgia) to rope my life in by His love and acceptance.

The Voice

One day, Jack asked me to go to lunch with him at the Snack Bar. It was full of G.I.s rushing around trying to get their meals before they had to get back to work or into the village for fun. Jack made sure that the conversation got around to God. I wasn't afraid to talk about God, as I had many conversations over the years that did not make me feel too trapped or persuaded to change. We talked about many things religious like but soon got around to God Himself. Turning to Jack, I commanded, "Explain the Trinity to me!"

Now, the topic of the Trinity can be hard to understand for many people, but Jack didn't seem to be bothered by the question. He explained to my satisfaction God the Father, the Son and then the Holy Spirit. When he said, "Well, the Holy Spirit is God's presence in the earth today," I heard someone speak behind me. *"Listen to this man, for what he is saying is true!"*

A literal voice, spoken right behind my right ear, speaking softly and declaring words that would shake me, direct me, and slowly woo me to the answers of the acceptance I desired. It was weird, scary, and very unnerving! The place was full of human beings going about their daily routines, unaware, or uncaring of Specialist Fifth Class Murl Edward Gwynn. I turned to see who was speaking. No one there! What or who could it have been, speaking down into the very depths of my soul and saying, "Listen to this man, for what he is saying is true!"

I wanted to get up and run, but something or someone was pulling at my heart, which craved for more of this life saving information. Jack, knowing that something had happened, spoke up, "What's the matter?"

"Nothing! I just thought someone said something!" I replied! We ended the meal, conversation, and my first encounter with Life Himself.

The Prayer

Going about my life after the "The Voice" experience seemed to be anticlimactic, to say the least. As a matter of fact, I was into the darkest times of my life. The village was my second home when I was not on duty. Drinking heavily, doing some drugs, and being with prostitutes were my nightly fix. Although now I am embarrassed over that time in my life, I have come to realize that my story is like many others who were in the military and away from their spouses. The pull of sex, booze, and the many other deadly desires of mankind's sinful nature come from one source... Godlessness.

Jack knew that I was living like the devil, but still had time for me. He was a friend, even though officers were not supposed to fraternize with enlisted men. He took time with me and every opportunity he could he spoke "Jesus" to me. I listened to Jack and Bill's life's lessons of living reality and stuck close to their invitations. They were sensitive to the direction of the Holy Spirit and did not crowd or pressure me.

The evening they invited me to Jack's room was not out of the ordinary. Sometimes officers would have enlisted men over to their rooms, but it was not usual. I didn't think much of it, as I could flow pretty well with people. They wanted to have a snack in Jack's room, so okay! We ate, talked about work and soon talked about God. After a few minutes, they were asking about my life and the lifestyle I was living. I didn't hold anything back and even up-held it like it was something to be proud of. Obviously, they weren't impressed and informed me that God was not happy with that type of life. Jack gently informed me that God made a way for my sins and shortcomings to be taken care of and that that way was Jesus, who died for them.

At the moment of hearing about Jesus and His dying for my sins, I felt guilty and condemned. They told me what I needed to do was to ask Jesus into my life and ask for forgiveness for my many sins. I bowed my head and prayed! "God, forgive me, Jesus take my life!" I repeated his prayer and didn't feel any different. It didn't make much of an impact on me then. In fact, I went back to the village that same night.

Mid-Tour Leave

At the mid-point in my one year assignment in Korea, or mid-tour, I was authorized a thirty day leave. I had the days and was soon on my way home to see Ruth, Dana, and family. This thirty day leave would be used to plant another nail in the coffin of the soon dead, old Murl Gwynn.

How great it was being with Ruth! She looked wonderful and even more beautiful than before. We spent the time at her parents' house, as that is where she was staying while I was away. We talked, played with Dana, and shopped. Fargo was not too far away so we went into the city and looked around. At West Acres Mall I bought a book that would scare me and be used to inform me that there was a God that everyone must give an account to.

As we walked around the mall checking out the many shops, my eye was attracted to this one bookstore. At the front of the store was the best seller at that time, "The Late Great Planet Earth", by Hal Lindsey. I didn't know that it was religious in nature nor that it spoke of the end times, but I bought it. Buying a book for me was completely out of the ordinary. It seemed right, however, buying that book. No matter that I had a very hard time reading anything. No matter that I had not bought a book before that time. No matter that reading was nothing I wanted to do. I just bought it!

The next day, after waking from a wonderful sleep next to Ruth, I picked up the book and began to read. Halting, picking up words, fighting my diction and grammar, I made it through that book. Hours later, still in bed I was scared, frustrated and confused. What if the information in this book was real? If Jesus was coming again to judge the world and cleanse it of sin, I was in trouble! I put the book down and spent the rest of my leave time enjoying Ruth and Dana.

Our time together went very fast and it seemed like I had just gotten home when I had to depart. It was hard saying goodbye to Ruth again, but I had no choice. I was a soldier!

The Lesson

This chapter's lesson: If you are a Christian, you have a responsibility to unsaved people. No born-again person has a right to his/her own life, once he/she are saved it belongs to Jesus. Jack and Bill lived that reality. By being obedient to Jesus' command to "go and tell," they opened up the unseen world of Christ to the felt world of Murl Gwynn. Jack and Bill lived a life that was spiritual and it affected the natural and released supernatural ability around them. They glowed with the presence of heaven. Their spiritual conversation was confirmed by the voice of God, and their fervent prayers arrested my attention and brought me to life Himself. **Matt 5:13 Ye are the salt of the earth: but if the salt have lost his savour, wherewith shall it be salted? it is thenceforth good for nothing, but to be cast out, and to be trodden under foot of men. 14 Ye are the light of the world. A city that is set on an hill cannot be hid. 15 Neither do men light a candle, and put it under a bushel, but on a candlestick; and it giveth light unto all that are in the house. 16 Let your light so shine before men, that they may see your good works, and glorify your Father which is in heaven.**

Chapter Six

A New Life-Accepted

Getting back to Korea was the beginning of the last part of my tour. I had six months to go and I was determined to make the best of it, even if I hated it. Taking tours of the Korean countryside, traditional Korean cultural events, and helping in a small orphanage took up some of those six months. It was interesting learning what made these people who they were. I wanted to know them, but found breaking the habit of the bars and prostitutes was harder than one would think.

I often went to the NCO Club, lined up three dollars' worth of dimes and told the bartender to give me as many drinks as dimes, as it would be dime a drink night. I got drunk, obnoxious, and sick. At no time, however, did I ever think I had had too much. After drinking at the NCO club, just before curfew[18], I hurried off the base and into the village to find a prostitute for the night

---

[18] Curfew was 12AM, if we were found on the streets past that time, we would be taken to jail.

and bed. I woke up many mornings in a prostitute's bed.

What a dark, nightmarish life I was in. Drinking, prostitutes, and inner hate made my existence unbearable most of the time. I wanted a change, but didn't know what to do, as there was this constant tugging of my flesh for more of the impure.

Meeting Him

It was August 1972 and I had just come back from the village, early for a change. It was a hot night, and I was drunk and tired. I just wanted my bed. There was some kind of a party going on in the barracks, as I could hear the noise, music, and cursing as I approached the front door. I could smell the sweet pungent smoke of marijuana slowly filtering down the steps and into the nostrils of any passerby. Whoever was partying heard me coming and told everyone to be quiet, but when they realized it was me, they welcomed my presence. Not wanting to party anymore that night, I took a joint of "dope" and retired to my room.

It had been one of those days and nights when I had been thinking of Ruth and what her life displayed. I knew she was not going out on me, like I was on her. I thought about the book I had read while on leave, which caused me to realize that if Jesus would return, if there was a

Jesus, that I surely wouldn't be ready to meet Him. Flopping down on my bed, I recalled the day Jack and I were in the Snack Bar and the voice. My mind was screaming as I thought about those words I repeated in Jack's room months before..."Jesus, come into my life and forgive my sins." The words seemed to be very appropriate now, and this time they came from my very total being, not just my mind. **"God, I am making a mess of my life. I have sinned against you, Ruth and many others. I believe in you, and if there is a Jesus, and He died for my sins, please forgive me. Jesus, come into my life!"**

I felt so very funny, not the type of funny that makes you laugh, but funny in the sense that says "Something is different!" I sensed a presence in my room; it was Jesus, I just knew it! He came over to my bed, reached down and grabbed me with both hands by my chest and pulled. I felt this power come over me, yanking at the center of my existence and wrenching at my sin, dark flesh, and waywardness. I was free! I felt accepted! There was a cleansing in me that only God could provide.

Up until that time I could be in a room with Ruth, Dana, relatives, and friends and I always felt lonely. My life was like the cartoon of the guy walking down the street with a storm and dark cloud over only him. However, at the instant that Jesus grabbed my life, the loneliness was gone. The dark, stormy clouds of despair and inner rejection were gone. My mind was clear; I was sober, and wide-awake.

I jumped up from the bed and ran down the hall to Mike's cubicle. Something had happened to me and I just had to tell someone. Mike's window was open and the streetlight flowed into the room. "Mike, wake up, there is something I have got to tell you!" Mike rolled over onto his back, looked up into my face and before I could tell him what happened he said, "Don't tell me, you just met Jesus!"

I couldn't believe that the change was so evident, but apparently it was. There is scripture that states, **"Therefore if any man [be] in Christ, [he is] a new creature: old things are passed away; behold, all things are become new." (2Cor 5:17)** The "all things becoming new" had started at that very moment. Jesus was in me and I was His. I knew that my life was worth something and that the deadly self-loathing was over.

Changes

Changes took place every day. I found myself thinking good thoughts that were pure and wholesome. Prayer became a constant food for my soul and fed my flesh at moments of weakness. Instead of giving into the baser ways of life, I found that I could go to God for help and find relief from desires that I knew would pull me down.

I was the guy at the office who would lock up each night, but ever since I found my new life in Christ, I wanted to get out of there and back to my room to read the Bible Jack had given me. There is a month, to this day, that I cannot remember eating after work. I'm sure I did, but I can't remember it, as I would forget about eating and run to my room for prayer and scripture reading.

If someone would have told me that the "high" you get from being one of God's children is more peaceful than booze, drugs and women, I would have never believed him. I wanted to know Him more, learn about His ways, and constantly drink from His fountain of life. Nothing caught my attention like loving God's daily presence. I would slip however!

The Dog Returns to His Vomit

If you would have told me during the "high" times that I would have ever gone back to the village, I would have told you that you were on something. Learning is an important part of being a Christian. There is more to a walk with God than fuzzy, fun times and goose bump emotions. Even God's kids have down days and weak moments. I found mine about a month from the moment I turned it all over to Jesus.

Being away from home and the people you love can cause a person to become lonely, drained, and filled with self-pity. That is what happened to me one night. It had been a bad day, and I wanted companionship, but instead of going to God for comfort and joy, I went to the village for just "one" beer. One beer, when you are down, never satisfies the flesh, and you will crave more in order to drown the feelings. It led to other things! I learned a lesson, which I never forgot..."Never, but never, give in to your emotions. They will lead you in the wrong direction."

The village, after that one instance, never had that pull on me again. I spent my time doing things that would not distract from my faith and love of God. I drank some, but never to the point that I lost control.

Putting effort into my job, tours, and making things at the craft shop took up most of my time. Between Bible reading and study, I found that my interests were much broader than I imagined. I even found that I was learning to read better than before. Even though reading was not the greatest desire of my life, I knew that the life of Christ was found between the pages of the Bible. Read I did!

Write I did too! Before I had left for Korea I had told Ruth I would write to her every day. Because I was drunk most of the time, before Jesus, I would forget and then try to write her when I was drunk. It didn't work. After I found my life in Christ, I could write to Ruth without any guilt or remorse. She could read my letters somewhat better, but I still had a long way to go with grammar and diction.

Home

Departing Korea was easy. There were no touches of nostalgia or other warm fuzzes. Leaving was "good"! I knew that if there was any thing I would miss about Korea it would be my buddy, Mike Huttner. We said good-bye and hoped that we would see each other again sometime in the future. He went back to Minnesota and I to North Dakota. We would see each other many times after Korea.

Arriving in North Dakota was great. I had served my time in Korea and was ready for our new assignment at Ft. Bliss, in El Paso, Texas. We stayed for a short while at Ruth's parents and then we were off to Texas. We would be starting over, sort of speaking, in our marriage. I had a new life in Christ, things were looking up, and I was excited about what the future would hold.

The Lesson

What can you say? The lesson in this chapter is this; Jesus is the way, the truth and the life. Go to Jesus to find your way, the right way. Go to Jesus to receive the truth, the correct truth about anything or subject. Go to Jesus for your life, life that is worth something and that will last for eternity. **John 14:6 Jesus saith unto him, I am the way, the truth, and the life....**

Chapter Seven

New Things

Arriving in El Paso and Ft. Bliss with a wife and child was different this time. We soon found a house to rent about three miles from the Post[19] and put our names on the Military Quarters list. We lived in a good neighborhood and met our neighbors and got to know them.

My new job was in the training school area. Having just been promoted to Staff Sergeant, I was the Operations Sergeant, in charge of 400 military students. That job was fun and challenging as it tasked my reading skills, caused me to dig deep within myself for talents and courage, and forced me to give a hundred percent. I liked it!

We soon got into our new routine as a family and were settling into a somewhat normal lifestyle. Since my new life in Christ was still so fresh, and I wanted everything God had to offer, we found a little Baptist Church to attend.

---

[19] Post is the term for a military base.

Sunlight Baptist was the place where I got my spiritual feet wet and dug deep into the Bible. Brother Ware, the pastor, was a good pastor and taught me much. He knew Greek and set up a time for a friend, Bill Brammer, and me to study this language as it is used in scripture. It was fun!

Church became our second home. We were involved in everything within the church. Every church activity was our source of fun and family. I became, along with Bill Brammer, like a right hand man to the pastor. B.W. (B.W. was our name for the pastor, short for Brother Ware.) taught us much and installed a deep sense of the importance of God's word. It was from B.W. that I learned to seek out the scripture for myself and not to trust anyone for its truths. Thanks, B.W.!

The Drink

Although our new life was going along very well, I still was drinking whiskey, the residue of the past. I didn't get drunk, but I bought a Fifth quite often. The booze had a hold on me and I knew it. I would take a drink of whiskey, feel bad about it, and then pour the remainder down the drain. The next day, on my way home from work I would buy another Fifth. I was going broke and crazy from this weekly routine. Something had to give!

Then one evening, just after taking a shot of booze, feeling guilty, and pouring the remainder down the drain, I cried out to God. "Lord, I can't handle this booze, I need your help. Please take the craving for this stuff away!" I felt free, and for some reason I knew that the booze did not have a hold on me anymore. That was in 1973, and to this day I am free from the addiction of booze. Jesus took it away when I gave it up!

If you are reading this and have a problem with booze, then let me encourage you. You can be free from booze or any other addiction only by completely surrendering it to Jesus. You can't and won't do it by yourself. Jesus died to completely set mankind free from anything that is not of God. He has the power, ability, and know-how to cleanse, mend, and straighten your life out. **John 8:36 If the Son therefore shall make you free, ye shall be free indeed.**

There are thousands of churchgoers[20] who struggle with alcohol, drugs, and other illicit items of the flesh. It is important to examine your life, to see if you are truly in the faith. Not just a churchgoer, but also a true born-again believer. Church is good, and we must go to church for fellowship, strengthening, and instruction, but we must not let that determine if we are really God's child. Only a total sold out

---

[20] I call these people churchgoers other than Christians because a true disciple of Jesus would not willfully partake of those things on a continual basis.

attitude of heart and mind can usher a person into the Kingdom of God. **2Cor 13:5 Examine yourselves, whether ye be in the faith; prove your own selves. Know ye not your own selves, how that Jesus Christ is in you, except ye be reprobates?**

I guess a fair question that you could ask me here is, "Have you had temptations, since you poured that drink down the drain and asked for God's help?" Yes, I have! Being changed by Jesus does not make us immune from temptations. Temptation is always present with all humans, Christian or not. When the temptations come, we must learn to run to a source that has power over them; that source is Jesus! **1Cor 10:13 There hath no temptation taken you but such as is common to man: but God [is] faithful, who will not suffer you to be tempted above that ye are able; but will with the temptation also make a way to escape, that ye may be able to bear [it].**

I have found that if I keep my thoughts on Christ, study the Bible daily, and fellowship with other Christians, the temptations do not stand a chance to germinate in my heart, soul and mind.

The Prophet

Being an Operations Sergeant put me in contact with soldiers from all walks of life, color, and age. Their every administrative need, as well as their class schedule, was my responsibility. You name it, and I did it! I met all students, directed their daily routines, and informed them of any calls, important changes, and upcoming events.

I took advantage of my association with each soldier. When they would come into my office, I would find ways to get the conversation around to Jesus and their need for a changed life. Many soldiers laughed at me, called me "The Prophet," and ignored my suggestions and interventions. They would smile and pretend to listen, but I knew they could care less. Hundreds did care less, but there were many who would succumb to the wooing of the Holy Spirit through me. In times of personal crises, many would "come by" the "Office."

And "come by" the "Office" they did! I could always tell when they wanted to talk. They would step in front of my office door, look down the hall both ways to see if anyone was watching, and then ask, "Sergeant Gwynn, could I talk to you about something personal?" I knew it had nothing to do with school or the Army; it was wife, family, or friend-related. I would ask the clerks to find something else to do and then invite the "Searching Soul" into my lair.

Many a soldier came face to face with their lost life in my office. They would cry, moan, and wring their hands. Some would get mad as I told them the answer to their questions. Some would change right there and then and walk away a new person. Some didn't know what they wanted and never found the answers. "The Prophet" was always available for anyone and would stay late to impart the life he had received in Korea. Thank you, Jesus! **Matt 11:28 Come unto me, all [ye] that labour and are heavy laden, and I will give you rest.**

Heart Murmur

I was happy, excited and learning some wonderful new things. Being a husband after meeting Jesus sure made things better in our marriage. Ruth was a different woman to me, although the one who had changed was me. I loved her and wanted to be with her often. That love was manifested in our second child, Tonya, who was born on January 21st, 1974.

Tonya was cute, cuddly, and blue. After a very quick and normal delivery Tonya was placed in intensive care because she turned a bluish color when she received her first bottle. The doctor checked her out and found that she had a defective valve in her heart. If the valve would not correct itself before she was six months old, she would have to have open-heart surgery.

Our trust was completely in God. Although we were new at trusting God for everything, we knew that God could heal Tonya's heart. At the end of the fifth month we went for a walk around our neighborhood and prayed. Up one street and then down another we went, praying, crying, and calling out to God. "Lord, we know you know all things, and You know what's wrong with Tonya's heart...You made it. We ask You to heal it, in Jesus name, Amen!" **Prov 3:5 Trust in the LORD with all thine heart; and lean not unto thine own understanding. 6 In all thy ways acknowledge him, and he shall direct thy paths.**

The next day as we went to the hospital for her final crucial checkup, there was peace in our hearts. Sure, we were nervous, but there was a peace that passed understanding. Our doctor confirmed that Tonya's heart was okay; however, she had a small "heart murmur." We were elated and went home with Tonya, our faith bolstered, and prepared for new adventures with Jesus.

Korea Again

Life was going great; I had a great job, Tonya was healed, the booze wasn't a problem, I felt accepted and clean, and the future looked bright. The bright future was overcast by a call into the Captain's office one day, however. I didn't see it coming and never in my wildest dreams had I thought that I would have to face something like that again. The C.O.[21] had just received new assignment notifications, and my name was on the list for Korea. Korea. Man, I just got back from there and if I never went back it would be too soon! Sure, it was the place that I had met Jesus and my life was made right, but outside of that, I did not want to go back to the many temptations and separation from Ruth and children.

As I walked into the house, or should I say as I crawled into the house from work that day, I must have looked like I had been slapped in the face with a smelly washrag. After telling Ruth the bad news, we went into the bedroom, laid down on the bed and cried. We talked, cried, talked and then prayed. "Oh, Lord, here we are again, needing your help. I don't want to go back to Korea. However, if you want me there for some reason, so be it! But, God, we are asking you to do something and change this thing. Thank you, in Jesus name!"

The next day I went to the C.O. and told him my heart's desires. He said that there probably wasn't anything he could do, but he would try. I went over to the Personnel Office and talked to whoever would listen. Everyone told me that I would probably have to go to Korea. I told everyone that I would go to Korea only if that is where God wanted me, and if that were so, I

---

[21] C.O. is the acronym for Commanding Officer

would go gladly. My heart told me that I was not to go back to Korea. The assignment people said that there might be assignments in Germany, but I would have to go in a very short time. I said okay! We didn't debate or question, we just got ready to go to Germany.

We now know that the assignment to Korea question came from the enemy of our souls. After going to Germany and experiencing the many things that transpired there we realized that God had many powerful things for us and Korea would have thwarted those realities. Many times since, we have seen the hand of Satan trying to dissuade or redirect something God was directing. It is for those reasons that the Christian must be sensitive to the leading of the Holy Spirit; otherwise he could be thrown off course for Christ.

It was 1974 and we were on our way to Germany. Would we have gone if we had known what was in store for us?

The Lesson

Circumstances can test your faith, get your attention or throw you off course. How you deal with the circumstances is in your hands. God has a purpose and plan for you, but what you do with testing times is in your ballpark. Faith, if it is not tested and tried, becomes dead religion. I think it is very important to learn through every circumstance. We must not become complacent in our faith. Learn to expect the trying of your faith, the testing of your fortitude, and the exercising of your will. This is Godly and necessary for proper growth. **1Pet 1:6 Wherein ye greatly rejoice, though now for a season, if need be, ye are in heaviness through manifold temptations: 7 That the trial of your faith, being much more precious than of gold that perisheth, though it be tried with fire, might be found unto praise and honour and glory at the appearing of Jesus Christ: 8 Whom having not seen, ye love; in whom, though now ye see [him] not, yet believing, ye rejoice with joy unspeakable and full of glory: 9 Receiving the end of your faith, [even] the salvation of [your] souls.**

Chapter Eight

Adventures in Faith

The two NCOs met me at Rein Main Air Base on a chilly German evening. Nice guys they were; made me feel very welcome to Germany and informed me of everything from my new assignment to the dollar/mark conversion rate. We immediately departed the Air Base, got on the Autobahn[22] and headed for Wurzburg, Germany.

They talked all the way to Wurzburg, I think to overcome any embarrassment of meeting the newbie. When I could get a word in, I asked questions about my duty section, who my immediate commanding officer would be and what my job would be.

The answer to who my immediate commanding officer would be floored me! The Sergeant described Major Miller, the S3 Officer for whom I would be working. "Well, he is a very nice guy. He doesn't hassle people, always tries to help, never gets upset and gets along with everybody in the office. He doesn't drink, smoke or mess around, I would say he is a Christian!"

---

[22] The Germany Interest Highway.

"He is a Christian?" That grabbed my attention! I had been praying for a Christian boss! Thank you Jesus, if this is true!

The reason I was so impressed by this Sergeant's answer is because they both were using many words in the conversation that caused the air to stink. This led me to believe that they were not believers, which was supported over the years I served with them.

We arrived at the Headquarters of the 69th Group at Emmery Casern. It was late and as we walked up the steps to the barracks/office building, I noticed a Bible sitting on the desk of the CQ[23]. Sergeant Purcell, a young Sergeant, was sitting in the chair with his feet up watching us come in.

"Sergeant Purcell, this is Sergeant Gwynn."

"Nice to meet you!"

"Same here!" "Say, whose Bible is that?"

"Why that's mine" said Sgt. Purcell "Why?"

"Well, I have one just like it."

"You do?"

"Yes, I am a believer and love Jesus, how about you?"

Looking surprised at the newbies boldness, Sgt. Purcell smiled, grabbed my hand and proudly said, "Welcome, Brother!"

---

[23] CQ is the acronym for Charge of Quarters, who is in charge for the night in case of emergencies. It usually is a night of pure torture for anyone who has the duty, trying to keep awake.

With that, I was introduced to the beginning of what would become one great faith adventure in Germany.

The next morning, I was escorted into the office of Major William Miller[24], my new boss. As soon as the Sergeant Major closed the door I made a statement. "Sir, before you say anything, I would like to say something."

"Go ahead, Sgt. Gwynn."

"Sir, I want you to know that I love Jesus with my whole heart, that I am born-again and that I live for God."

What happened next surprised me as I was not expecting this Officer to respond the way he did. Usually, officers have a tendency to be aloof to NCOs. Not Maj. Miller, he was/is a down to earth kind of guy, I really liked him. He stood to his feet, raised his arms in the air, and shouted,

"Praise the Lord, I have been praying for a Christian NCO in this section!"

I had just been welcomed to my new job. What a job!

We talked for a long time. He told me about the duties I would be assigned to, the living conditions and housing for our family, and the church and family of believers in that area. I told him about my background, and my marriage, and how I met Jesus. It was exciting and really different, as I had never met an officer

---

[24] William Miller retired as a Full Colonel.

(other than Jack and Bill in Korea) who loved Jesus and wasn't afraid to talk about Him. I opened up to him and shared many things that at the time I didn't realize would be used to usher me into a greater walk with God.

Cell Group

Ruth was still in the States and wouldn't be coming until I got a place for us to live. Military housing was in short supply, and we had to wait for our name to come to the top of the list. I found an apartment on the economy[25] and settled in until Ruth could come.

Maj. Miller had a Cell Group in his home once a week and invited me to attend. I took him up on the invitation and went on a Thursday evening.

A Cell Group is a group of Christians who met for Bible Study, fellowship, and support. The term "Cell" comes from the concept of a human cell in the body. The human body is made up of cells, which in turn make up organs and then the whole body. The "Cell Group" pattern itself after the human cell by each member, as an individual, working together and then making up the Church in that particular local. The Cell Group is a tremendous tool in

---

[25] This was civilian housing.

the Church to make every participant feel welcome, supported, and needed.

At Maj. "Bill" Miller's Cell Group the first night I was introduced to the power of the Holy Spirit. As the bible study progressed through the night, I noticed an older man in the group staring at me. It made me uneasy and concerned about what I may have gotten into. Maybe I was not welcome in this group as much as I thought I was.

After the singing, teaching, sharing, and prayer, the "starer" came over to me and was introduced as Bob Westmoreland. This "starer" became a mentor, trusted friend, and faithful brother in the Lord. After the introductions, Bill told me to tell Bob what I had shared with him in his office that first day.

I was embarrassed by Bill's request, as what I had shared with him was embarrassing to me and I thought was my own business and not open for public knowledge. I had shared with Bill because I felt so comfortable with him. But to share it with this guy I hardly knew, in that setting, was something else. However, I shared the following with him.

Back in El Paso I had gone to a bookstore one day and bought the book "They Speak With Other Tongues", by John Sherrill. The book is an essay about John Sherill's quest to understand the phenomenon of "speaking in tongues." This phenomenon is spoken about in scripture many places throughout the New Testament. You can see those instances in the following passages.

Mark 16:17 And these signs shall follow them that believe; In my name shall they cast out devils; they shall speak with new tongues;

Acts 2:2 And suddenly there came a sound from heaven as of a rushing mighty wind, and it filled all the house where they were sitting. 3 And there appeared unto them cloven tongues like as of fire, and it sat upon each of them. 4 And they were all filled with the Holy Ghost, and began to speak with other tongues, as the Spirit gave them utterance.

Acts 2:11 Cretes and Arabians, we do hear them speak in our tongues the wonderful works of God.

Acts 10:46 For they heard them speak with tongues, and magnify God. Then answered Peter, 47 Can any man forbid water, that these should not be baptized, which have received the Holy Ghost as well as we?

Acts 19:6 And when Paul had laid [his] hands upon them, the Holy Ghost came on them; and they spake with tongues, and prophesied.

1Cor 12:10 To another the working of miracles; to another prophecy; to another discerning of spirits; to another [divers] kinds of tongues; to another the interpretation of tongues: 11 But all these worketh that one and the selfsame Spirit, dividing to every man severally as he will.

1Cor 12:28 And God hath set some in the church, first apostles, secondarily prophets, thirdly teachers, after that miracles, then gifts of healings, helps, governments, diversities of tongues.

1Cor 14:4 He that speaketh in an [unknown] tongue edifieth himself; but he that prophesieth edifieth the church. 5 I would that ye all spake with tongues, but rather that ye prophesied: for greater [is] he that prophesieth than he that speaketh with tongues, except he interpret, that the church may receive edifying. 6 Now, brethren, if I come unto you speaking with tongues, what shall I profit you, except I shall speak to you either by revelation, or by knowledge, or by prophesying, or by doctrine?

1Cor 14:21 In the law it is written, With [men of] other tongues and other lips will I speak unto this people; and yet for all that will they not hear me, saith the Lord. 22 Wherefore tongues are for a sign, not to them that believe, but to them that believe not: but prophesying [serveth] not for them that believe not, but for them which believe. 23 If therefore the whole church be come together into one place, and all speak with tongues, and there come in [those that are] unlearned, or unbelievers, will they not say that ye are mad? 24 But if all prophesy, and there come in one that believeth not, or [one] unlearned, he is convinced of all, he is judged of all: 25 And thus are the secrets of his heart made manifest; and so falling down on [his] face he will worship God, and report that God is in you of a truth. 26 How is it then, brethren? when ye come together, every one of you hath a psalm, hath a doctrine, hath a tongue, hath a revelation, hath an interpretation. Let all things be done unto edifying. 27 If

any man speak in an [unknown] tongue, [let it be] by two, or at the most [by] three, and [that] by course; and let one interpret. 28 But if there be no interpreter, let him keep silence in the church; and let him speak to himself, and to God.

1Cor 14:39 Wherefore, brethren, covet to prophesy, and forbid not to speak with tongues. 40 Let all things be done decently and in order.

Mark 16:17 And these signs shall follow them that believe; In my name shall they cast out devils; they shall speak with new tongues;

Well, I bought the book, read it through, checked out its accuracy in the scriptures and decided the Baptism in the Holy Spirit was for me. You see, tongues were a manifestation given to the believers throughout the New Testament after the Holy Spirit came upon them and then resided in them.

It was a warm sunny day, Ruth was in the kitchen and Dana and Tonya were either sleeping or playing. I went back to our bedroom, closed the door, flipped through the book by John Sherrill, decided it was right that I seek the Baptism of the Holy Spirit and prayed. "Dear Lord, I know I am your child. You have set me free and saved me. I believe the Baptism of the Holy Spirit is for all believers. Please baptize me in the Holy Spirit. Thank You!" I looked in the mirror, opened my mouth like it said in scripture "They shall speak with new tongues." and waited for the words to come. Nothing happened, so I opened my mouth and yelled "Blaw!" Still nothing happened, but I felt like an idiot, looking at myself in the mirror with my mouth wide open. I must be doing something wrong. I decided that maybe it wasn't for me and started to depart the room.

I got to the door but couldn't get it open. Not that the door was locked or stuck, something in my being prevented me from departing that room. I fell to my knees next to the bed and prayed. "Lord, I don't understand all of this, and maybe I am making a mistake, but if there is any more to receive from you I want it, even if I have to stand on my head to get it!"

You can understand why I would be embarrassed to have other people know about the "mirror" experience; When Bill told me to tell Bob about that little mirror mimicking I felt silly to say the least. However, I told Bob the story.

Bob didn't laugh, make fun of me or act like it was silly. Instead of patting me on the back and making me feel okay he grabbed my Bible from under my arm and said, "Do you believe everything in this Bible?"

"Yes!"

"O.K., I am going to get you into a corner with your own Bible!" Then he proceeded to show me every place that scripture taught about the Baptism of the Holy Spirit and speaking in tongues. When he was finished, he said, "Do you believe those scriptures and if you do, do you want the same thing?"

I was going to say no, but remembered my prayer next to the bed that day..."I want anything from You, even if I have to stand on my head to receive it." I sat down, and Bob and Bill prayed for me to receive the Baptism in the Holy Spirit. I felt warm, light, a little light headed, but wonderful. No, I didn't speak in tongues, but that was soon to come.

I felt like I was lighter than a feather as I drove home that night. Everything seemed to be different. I knew that I had known Jesus before the events of this night, but for some reason He was more magnified in my whole being. I now know that the Holy Spirit magnifies Jesus in the believer. **John 16:13 (NIV) But when he, the Spirit of truth, comes, he will guide you into all truth. He will not speak on his own; he will speak only what he hears, and he will tell you what is yet to come. 14 He will bring glory to me by taking from what is mine and making it known to you.**

Sleeping that night was next to impossible as all I wanted to do was praise God and worship Him as my Lord and Master. I felt like I was floating two feet above my bed. I was happy, so very much in tune with God's Spirit, and wanted nothing more than to please Him.

Ruth Arrives

In a few months Ruth arrived from North Dakota. It was her first overseas airplane flight and one that tested her patience and stamina.

She came walking down the corridor with Tonya in her arms, Dana by her side and many people helping her out. She was tired, exhausted, and ready to just quit. Her flight was anything but fun. Who would have known that Tonya would start to cry the moment the airplane lifted off of the ground in the USA? The poor child cried the entire ten-hour flight to Germany. I guess everyone on board heard Tonya cry and fuss. Attendants and passengers all took their turns trying to calm the child down, with no results. Tonya cried the whole trip.

Ruth looked so good to me. How I had missed her! We gathered their suitcases, cleared customs, and piled into the VW I had brought with me from Texas. We talked and shared as we drove down the Autobahn looking at the sights of our new homeland.

It wasn't very far down the Autobahn that I blurted out, "I have been baptized in the Holy Spirit and speak in tongues!" Ruth looked at me, rolled her eyes, and said, "What?" You can imagine what she must have thought. Here she was, just had the nightmare flight from the Twilight Zone, and now stuck in a VW with a religious nut. You guessed it, I said, "What's the matter?" We guys just don't get it sometimes.

Telling Ruth about the tongues thing was dumb, to say the least. I should have waited. Being raised a Lutheran and told that the only ones who spoke in tongues were the crazies didn't help my proud acclamation to Ruth. I changed the subject and let it go for a later time and let God work on Ruth. She later was baptized in the Holy Spirit and now speaks in tongues.

The Lessons

It is important to be open to the leading of the Lord. What I learned during the early days in Germany was that God always has something new for us. When we think that we have God in a box, He jumps out and reveals His amazing bowl of fruitful love and His working gloves of spiritual gifts. He is always the same without ever being locked into man's way of thinking.

We need to stretch our faith and learn new things. There may be more to spiritual reality than what you are used to.

Acts 2:1 And when the day of Pentecost was fully come, they were all with one accord in one place. 2 And suddenly there came a sound from heaven as of a rushing mighty wind, and it filled all the house where they were sitting. 3 And there appeared unto them cloven tongues like as of fire, and it sat upon each of them. 4 And they were all filled with the Holy Ghost, and began to speak with other tongues, as the Spirit gave them utterance.

Chapter Nine

Ruth

Since the poor timing incident when Ruth arrived in Germany draws attention to the many things she had to put up with, now is the perfect time to devote a whole chapter to her. There are tremendous lessons to learn from her life. No person goes through what she went through without a solid foundation of spiritual truth. Ruth has that!

We settled into the new life in Germany. Living on the economy was fun, as we got to live like the average German. We lived in a little town called *Unterlinock*. It was a peaceful little village with friendly people and quiet neighborhoods. Our downstairs apartment was nice and cozy. Ruth enjoyed learning about the surrounding area and meeting the landlord.

We were getting along pretty well, but there was tension between us. Unbeknownst to me, Ruth was struggling with forgiving me for all the women, wild lifestyle and the general hurt that had come with all of those things.

I had been out in the field playing war games and had been gone about a week. When I got home, I could tell that Ruth was bothered about something, and I pressed her to tell me. She was reluctant to share what was on her mind, but I insisted, and she finally gave in with the problem.

While I was in the field, God had dealt with her about un-forgiveness toward me. He told her that my sins were under the blood of Christ and that I was forgiven, but her un-forgiveness towards me was putting her in danger of hell and that she must tell me and asked for my forgiveness.

She told me that she did not love me and that she had been lying about her feelings for me for a long time. She asked me to forgive her and that she had been trying to love me, but it wasn't working. I got angry and stormed off to the bedroom. I was hurt thinking that she didn't love me. "How could she treat me like that?" was all I could think of. Now, you can imagine the weird thinking that was going on here. I was the culprit that caused the pain and strife in our marriage, but I was forgiven. How could she? I told her that I would not live with someone who didn't love me, and that she could go back to her parent's house. I stayed In the bedroom for a while, sulking in my self-pity. Ruth went to the living room, sat on the couch and argued with God.

God was giving Ruth the heavy hand of love. She said to Him, "I told You that if I told him I didn't love him and had not forgiven him, he would send me back to North Dakota." God said, "Just wait a minute, it will be okay!" In a few minutes I came into the living room and said, "I'm sorry and understand why you felt that way. You had every reason to, but I think we can start over!" She looked at me, I at her, and we both knew that we could make our marriage work if we trusted God. We prayed and asked God to show us how to make it work. It worked!

The Lessons

Through the many heartaches and lonely nights of hurt, despair, and second thoughts, Ruth has learned much and has taught much in her own way.

Every married couple could learn from Ruth. The marriage vows she spoke to Murl Gwynn were sacred and precious. She knew that those vows were not only to Murl, but also to God. When she said "For better or worse" she meant every word. Words without action mean nothing, however. Her actions proved her heart. In this throw away age we live in, we all can learn from the Ruth's of this world.

In my ministry as a pastor and my trips throughout the world, I have met many who have had a similar story as mine. With each of those stories there is a "Ruth" on the receiving end of a "Murl"! Their story, whether man or woman, is never told, because many, sad to say, never stay around long enough to see the changed life of the troubled perpetrator.

I know now the hell Ruth went through. If I had been her, I probably would have killed me, or at the least divorced me. She didn't, and now stands out as one who trusted God.

Yes, I believe Ruth had the scriptural right to divorce me[26], but she made the greater choice of forgiveness. She professed to be a Christian, and God required her to live like it. Her life demonstrated the reality of forgiveness.

Was it easy? No! Could she have run? Yes! But what would have come of Murl Gwynn if she had run? I think her staying with me was the major link in my coming to Jesus. I think her staying with me has been used by God to touch other people in similar situations. We must remember, there is more to life than the proverbial "Me, Myself, and I." We all are

---

[26] Matt 19:7 (NIV) "Why then," they asked, "did Moses command that a man give his wife a certificate of divorce and send her away?" 8 Jesus replied, "Moses permitted you to divorce your wives because your hearts were hard. But it was not this way from the beginning. 9 I tell you that anyone who divorces his wife, except for marital unfaithfulness, and marries another woman commits adultery."

intertwined with each other; if we give up on one another, we may not have a chance.

What are we saying? We are saying, "If your marriage is not what it is supposed to be, run to God with your hurt, don't run away from your spouse." Please don't stay in a physically abusive situation. Get help immediately. However, if your marriage is not what you think it should be, divorce is not always the answer. If you will trust God for direction, strength, and love, He will give it. He knows your situation; let Him work in you, through you, and for your spouse. You're staying, even when it hurts, could be the lifesaving example to your spouse.

First Things First

The ability to stay in a marriage when everything seems to be going to hell comes from making the proper choices and having the right priorities. Ruth had the right priority!

When we lived in El Paso, just after Korea, I remember the night in our kitchen when I had to tell her something of great importance. My love for her was complete now, and I would do nothing to hurt her, but I had to make sure she understood my priorities.

"Honey, there is something I need to tell you."

"Yes, what is it?"

"What I am going to say may hurt you. I don't want to hurt you any more then I have in the past, but this is important."

"What is it?"

I told her about all the women, prostitutes, drugs and the many dirty things, without going into detail. She looked hurt, but handled the information with the understanding that every Christian should have and said, "I forgive you!"

Then I told her, "You know I love God now more than anything!"

"Yes!"

"I want you to know that God is first in my life and then you!" I was nervous and not sure what she would say. By now I should have known what her reply would be, but I wasn't sure.

She looked at me warmly and with no hesitation said, "I have always felt that way about God and you. Jesus is first, then you!" Wow, I was so happy. She felt the same way.

I humbly encourage anyone reading this to do what I did in telling Ruth about my past. There is the danger of hurt, deep sorrow, and a bad reaction from your spouse. However, if your marriage is founded upon truth, trust, and love now, it will stand the testing. You don't have to go into great detail, but share the sin, betrayal and shame. Be wise, sensitive to the Holy Spirit and lovingly understanding of their reaction. **Jame 5:16 Confess [your] faults one to**

another, and pray one for another, that ye may be healed.

Ruth's priorities in life were/are the foundational cement that caused her to stay with a husband who was living like the devil. God was number one, then husband and others. **Luke 14:26 If any [man] come to me, and hate not his father, and mother, and wife, and children, and brethren, and sisters, yea, and his own life also, he cannot be my disciple.**[27]

Every spouse needs to have that foundational priority. If God is number one, then everything else will flow from that relationship. God knows the future and what is needed in life to make a person strong, capable to withstand, and pliable in circumstances.

Husband Love Your Wife

Ruth has taught me much over the years. She has been a constant reminder to me of God's love, which is a never give up kind of love. Man, did I miss it early in our marriage by not knowing Jesus, not understanding His will for me or my responsibility in marriage.

Human marriage is a picture of God and His children. He wants us to know Him without

---

[27] Hate in this verse of scripture is not stating that you must actually hate those people, but that your love for God, in comparison, would be like hate.

anything that would keep that knowledge from flowing to us. Sin, obviously, blocks our relationship with Him. As we turn to the world and away from God, He in turn steps away because of our contamination of sin's filth. He wants intimacy, companionship, and a sharing of Himself and His life. We run away because we see Him as too far above us and too holy to commune with. Actually, our sin makes us unfit for relationship and companionship with God.

I said all that to say this. It is the husband's responsibilities to love, protect, and build up his wife. The husband should be the picture and example of Jesus to the wife. Jesus loves the church; husbands are to love their wives. Jesus builds up the church; husbands are to build up their wives. **Ephe 5:25 Husbands, love your wives, even as Christ also loved the church, and gave himself for it; 26 That he might sanctify and cleanse it with the washing of water by the word, 27 That he might present it to himself a glorious church, not having spot, or wrinkle, or any such thing; but that it should be holy and without blemish. 28 So ought men to love their wives as their own bodies. He that loveth his wife loveth himself. 29 For no man ever yet hated his own flesh; but nourisheth and cherisheth it, even as the Lord the church: 30 For we are members of his body, of his flesh, and of his bones. 31 For this cause shall a man leave his**

father and mother, and shall be joined unto his wife, and they two shall be one flesh. 32 This is a great mystery: but I speak concerning Christ and the church.

Ephe 5:33 Nevertheless let every one of you in particular so love his wife even as himself; and the wife [see] that she reverence [her] husband.

Through all the years that Ruth was not being loved, supported, and taken care of, she loved and reverenced her husband in her own way. Now, I submit to you, that any woman in a similar situation could do the same thing. If Jesus is your Lord, first love, and the one you submit to first, then anything is possible in your marriage.

Thank you, Ruth, for staying! I love you!

Chapter Ten

Moving Right Along

By the end of 1974 things were moving right along: interesting, fast, and exciting.

Our daily lives were saturated with God's presence and fellowship with the saints. Wurzburg, military chapel, activities at Leighton Barracks, and the constant infusion of Holy Spirit activity made us vibrantly alive.

It seemed that every place we turned there was someone to talk to about God's love and saving grace. The V.W. Bug I brought with us from the states turned into a mini church, grotto, and confessional all wrapped up in one.

I turned that V.W. over to the Lord and told Him I would pick up anyone and tell them about Jesus. Every hitchhiker was fair game and fresh meat for my brand of evangelism. If, on the rare occasions that I would pass a hitchhiker and not stop, the V.W.'s engine would die until I promised to back up and pick up the would be child of God.

The number of people who met Jesus in that yellow and cream-colored "Bug" is beyond remembrance now. What an honor I had being God's ambassador in Germany.

Elder

The church we attended was made up of soldiers and civilians from the USA and Germany. Military chaplain Major Curry Vaughn led it. He was a great pastor, and teacher and solid in his beliefs. Not once in the three years I was with him did I see him waver or compromise for Christ. His leadership made for a strong group of believers and taught us how men and women of God acted and spoke.

About a year from the day I arrived in Germany and started attending the church at Leighton Barracks I was asked to become an Elder in the congregation. Needless to say, I was honored and nervous. To be a leader of God's people was scary, as I would be representing the King of Kings and Lord of Lords. To this day, I still have butterflies in my stomach before I preach and teach. To speak on behalf of God, in His presence, gives me cause for seriousness and concern.

Nathan

A lot of wonderful things happened in Germany, too many to give an account here. Suffice it to say, God did marvelous, mysterious, and masterful things there. We saw lives changed, spiritual battles won, and devilish emissaries defeated. Our prayers would be answered in wonderful ways and we would see the challenges of faith produce realities that only God could materialize.

After three years in Germany, we knew we would soon be leaving for new horizons. We didn't know where or when, but we knew it would soon be coming.

About that time I began to pray for a son. Although we were happy with our daughters, I wanted a son. Dana and Tonya were happy exciting children, and watching them grow in the Lord made my heart warm. But a son would be nice too!

On a night that was quiet, cool and starlit I spoke to God about a son. I walked down the tree-lined street praying, seeking, and addressing my Master as to His will for a son. "Father, I know you have given me much and have blessed me beyond my wildest dreams. You have saved me, changed me and called me to do your will. If I am living my life and doing those things that give you pleasure, grant me a son. Thank you, in Jesus name!" That was it, I had asked, and I knew He would answer in His time and way!

About two months after the "prayer walk," as I was departing for work one day, Ruth stopped me at the door. She handed me a small cup and told me to take it to the hospital and have the contents analyzed. Being a male and obviously ignorant to what was handed me, I asked, "Why, what is it?" Ruth looked at me lovingly and said, "It is my urine. I think I'm pregnant!"

Pregnant! Could it be a son on his way? I was elated and nervous as I took the cup with its precious contents to the hospital to be analyzed. "How long will it take to get the results?" I asked the nurse.

"Sometime around noon!" came the reply.

Voice Two

Around noon, alone in my office, I called the hospital and asked the nurse what the results were on Ruth Gwynn's pregnancy test. It took the nurse about five minutes before she gave me the answer, "It is positive. Your wife is pregnant!"

"You will have a son and you are to call him Nathaniel!" That was the audible voice I heard in my office as I hung up the phone. It startled me and caused me to look around the office for the body connected to the voice; there was none.

I had heard God's voice for the second time, the first time being in Korea.

A son! Nathaniel! "Praise the Lord!" I didn't question the voice and faithfully trusted in the fact that we would have a son. I rushed home and told Ruth the good news. She too was excited and from that moment on we called our unborn child "Nathan"! There was no question in our hearts that we would have a son and told every one of our upcoming blessing. Sure, there were people who thought we were nuts, but we didn't care. Many nights I would speak to and read the Bible to Nathan in Ruth's womb.

7/7/77

"Honey, this is Ruth. You had better come right home; Nathan is ready to be born!" Ruth's voice on the phone told me that I had better hurry. I rushed down the steps, missing a few along the way, ran to the "Grotto on wheels," and sped home around the traffic circle, dodged many speeders like myself, turned right on the main drive paralleling the river and leading to my house. It was a beautiful day, the sun was shining, and the castle on the hill stood out like a beacon proclaiming, "Murl and Ruth are having Nathan!"

Nathan will be born soon, was all I could think of. What will he look like? How long will Ruth be in labor? I hope they will let me into the delivery room, was going through my mind. "Thank you Lord for this child, thank you for Nathan!" Just then in my spirit, soul, and mind I heard the still small voice that asked, "What day is it?"

"It's Thursday."

"But, what day is it?"

"It's Thursday, July seventh!"

"But, son, what DAY is it?"

Then it hit me, it was July seventh, nineteen hundred and seventy seven. All of the newspapers and radios were broadcasting that 7/7/77 was upon us and it was something special.

Within me again I heard the still, small voice, "What day is it?"

"It's July seventh, nineteen hundred and seventy seven!"

"Yes," said the voice, "and this is your confirmation that you heard from me, that you would have a son." The number seven in scripture indicates completion and perfection. This was God's confirmation to everyone that Nathan was ordained of God.

Nathan was born at seventeen hundred hours (5PM) on July seventh, nineteen hundred and seventy seven. He is a blessing to his mother and me and is now married. There is a calling upon his life that God will confirm in His timing.

The remainder of the time in Wurzburg was taken up in work, Bible studies and the chapel.

I was asked to give a teaching our last night at the chapel I don't remember what I taught on, but I do remember sitting there, recalling all of the wonderful spiritual things that had happened. Our life had been full, rich, and very exciting with the saints at Leighton Barracks and the chapel activities. There were so many people that had come to Christ from our efforts that we couldn't count them. Thank you, Jesus!

The Lesson

What is the lesson in the account of Nathan? Well, the main lesson is that God is interested in everything that happens in His children's lives. No detail, no happening, and no event are too small for God to be involved in. We must learn to trust Him for everything, look for Him to be involved, and expect things to work according to His plan. **Psalm 37:4 Delight thyself also in the LORD; and he shall give thee the desires of thine heart.**

Chapter Eleven

For I know the thoughts that I think toward you, saith the LORD, thoughts of peace, and not of evil, to give you an expected end. Jere 29:11

Ministry

We were back in the United States and looking forward to our new assignment at White Sands Missile Range, New Mexico.

White Sands was another confirmation of God's leading and blessings. While in Germany we made friends with Frank and Pat Albert. He and I were both ordained Elders at Leighton Chapel. We laughed, prayed together, played together and our wives got pregnant at the same time...that is how close we were. When it came time to depart Germany, we prayed about staying together in our new assignments. Although we didn't know it at the time we prayed, God fixed it so we would stay together at White Sands Missile Range. Not only would we be together at White Sands, we would be assigned to the same unit, same duty section, and "literally" the same office at the same desk. "Really!" If Frank needed to work at the desk I would have to find something else to do, and vice versa. What a wonderful God we serve.

Frank and I led many soldiers to the Lord. We had Bible studies in our homes and learned the great joy of being teachers and ministers of the gospel everywhere we went in that area.

Get Out

Our time at White Sands passed quickly as our time was taken up not only with our duty assignments but also with church at Las Cruces. Frank and I became elders at the Church of The Crosses and were busy spreading the gospel through every means. We were involved with radio, magazines, T.V. and just about any other media you could think of. It was most rewarding.

I was ready to stay in the Army until my twenty years were up, but God had other plans. One day at our church, after hearing Syvelle Phillips with Evangel Bible Translators (EBT) speak, I knew that God was calling me into the "full time" ministry. I didn't know when or how, but I knew I wanted to be a pastor.

Ruth, our children, and I went to Eagle River, Wisconsin, and "The Masters Haven" to learn more about EBT. EBT had a missionary training school at "The Masters Haven" which helped would-be missionaries learn more about their "calling." After one week I knew that God was calling us out of the Army, and into EBT. I wasn't sure what we would do, but God did.

Syvelle asked me what we wanted to do. I stated that I thought that God was calling us out of the Army and into EBT and that I wanted to put the Bible onto cassette tapes in the languages of the world. We had heard a minister share about his ministry with the North American Indians and putting the Bible into their language onto cassette tapes. EBT would be starting a division that would do the same thing. I was interested in that division.

Syvelle startled me when he said, "How would you like to join EBT and start the 'Recording Division?" Surprised and scared, I told him we would pray about it. The next day, after prayer, we confirmed that we would join and start the Recording Division. We were preparing to burn a bridge.

Talk about difficult! The day we drove off the military installation at White Sands was a tough day. The Army had become a home to us. It was safe, secure, and always very rewarding. Being a soldier, after I came to the Lord, put me into situations and areas that called upon every talent and gift I had. I used whatever the Lord gave me to reach soldiers for Christ. My dream was to be a Sergeant Major so that by the virtue of that rank I would have the ear of any soldier. By departing the Army, that dream would die. I had to weigh the cost, accept the consequence, and trust God. Either I had heard or not! I believed I had heard, so we departed. As we drove down the road from the Post, I had to stop the car, get out, and adjust the outside mirrors so that I could not look back. **Luke 9:62 And Jesus said unto him, No man, having put his hand to the plough, and looking back, is fit for the kingdom of God.** It was 1980.

Pastor

We moved to Dallas and began our ministry with EBT. We had to help remodel a building, learn about the recording ministry, construct a sound proof recording studio, and travel to other countries. Everything was new, exciting and taxing. We were involved with things we knew nothing about and had to learn, learn, and learn. Learn we did, though!

I learned how the recording was done, what would and would not work in a foreign setting and how to conduct oneself with people of other cultures. With all of this knowledge I put together a training course for missionaries who wanted to use the recording skills in their mission field. The "Recording Missionary" training manual has been used in Mexico, Peru, South Africa, and Sri Lanka.

By 1983 we had put together the Recording Division of EBT, but we sensed God telling us to depart EBT and start our own ministry called Harvest of Life. Harvest of Life would be a recording ministry much the same as the Recording Division of EBT.

EBT is still ministering in the bible translation field and touching thousands for Christ. Under the leadership of Syvelle and Lovie Phillips, EBT has been instrumental in helping many individuals begin their full-time ministry. Thank you, Syvelle and Lovie!

On one of my speaking tours through Georgia, I stopped in Cobbtown, Georgia, to visit Pastor Paul and Patty Longgrear. The Longgrears were with us in Germany in the 70's. I was an Elder with Paul at Leighton Chapel. Paul now pastored Christian Life Fellowship (CLF).

Paul asked me to stay the night and preach for him Sunday evening, as he would have to preach at another church across the state. I accepted and shared our ministry. Nothing unusual happened during the meeting, but the next day after I departed for Dallas, something did.

I was about a hundred miles away from Cobbtown when I heard a voice in the back seat. Please, I am not nuts; I am just sharing what happened. I know many people will say, "This guy sure hears voices a lot." That is what happened; period. Any way, I heard this voice say, "Light House Ministries from Elizabeth City, North Carolina, will call and ask you to be the Master of Ceremonies for a telethon. You are to do it. Also, you will become the pastor of Christian Life Fellowship in Cobbtown, Georgia."

Wow! I heard the voice, looked around and drove on. When I got home around midnight, I woke Ruth and told her about the voice. She looked surprised and said, "Light House Ministries called tonight about nine o'clock and asked if you would be the Master of Ceremonies for their telethon." Confirmation number one! In a month's time Paul called and asked if God had given me any new direction in my ministry. I told him yes, but what was it he called about? He stated that he was moving to that church he had preached at the night I was with them in Cobbtown and every time he prayed about who should be CLF's new pastor, my name always came to mind. "Had God spoken anything to me?" I told him about the voice in the car. That was that. We went to Cobbtown, I preached, and it was confirmed that I was to be the new pastor for Christian Life Fellowship.

We moved to Cobbtown and I became the pastor of CLF on August 13th, 1983. We are still here as of this writing, September 2013. I know

I am accepted, forgiven, and gifted. Are there lessons? Yes...read on!

Chapter Twelve

Accepted

It is now 2001 and a lot has happened with that young boy from Carrington, North Dakota. Time has made its impact on thinking, decision-making, and choices of the heart. There is no longer the need to be unduly accepted as my acceptance comes through Christ.

The dark avenues of human encounters that rob the heart of innocence have been detoured through the blood of the acceptable Lamb of God, Jesus. Having been detoured and arrested by God's love, there stands no reason for loathing or self-rejection. I am free, innocent and made right by Him who loved me before I knew Him.

If you have been tainted by circumstances that made you feel low, unworthy, or dirty, then listen to what this man says. There is a way for you to be free, cleansed and accepted. Jesus is the only way. It is not religion or churchy thinking. It is a complete surrender to Christ and His ways. You can't and won't be able to correct yourself. You need God.

Many people try church or religion without success. But you can't "try" God, you have to give up, give in and surrender. Surrendering makes you vulnerable and open to hurt, but this vulnerability can make you strong. The hurt will be salved with Christ's love and mercy. You will know and feel it in the inner person.

Being accepted in this life can be illusive because it is based upon other weak and human frailties. If we look to God for our acceptance, we will find peace and true encouragement of soul and mind. **Ephe 1:6 To the praise of the glory of his grace, wherein he hath made us accepted in the beloved.** He will direct us to Christ who was made acceptable on our behalf.

We must see beyond our immediate circumstances and daily routines to God's purpose for us. His desire is for everyone, including you, to be blessed and to know Him. He realizes that without His direct intervention we will miss the glorious life He wants us to have. **Ephe 1:3 Blessed [be] the God and Father of our Lord Jesus Christ, who hath blessed us with all spiritual blessings in heavenly [places] in Christ: 4 According as he hath chosen us in him before the foundation of the world, that we should be holy and without blame before him in love: 5 Having predestinated us unto the adoption of children by Jesus Christ to himself, according to the good pleasure of his will,**

Please understand that Jesus paid the price for every bad thing you ever thought, every bad action, and every bad meditation. God was pleased to kill Jesus on your behalf...**Isai 53:10 Yet it pleased the LORD to bruise him; he hath put [him] to grief: when thou shalt make his soul an offering for sin, he shall see [his] seed, he shall prolong [his] days, and the pleasure of the LORD shall prosper in his hand.** Anything you think is held against you has been taken care of in Christ; accept that truth! **Ephe 1:7 In whom we have redemption through his blood, the forgiveness of sins, according to the riches of his grace; 8 Wherein he hath abounded toward us in all wisdom and prudence; 9 Having made known unto us the mystery of his will, according to his good pleasure which he hath purposed in himself:**

You are not alone with shortcomings and problems. Every human is a sinner and needs help. Everyone must come to the same place that I came to; to the end of self and then turn to God.

If you have not turned to Jesus and His sacrifice on your behalf, then turn to Him now. Don't let another minute go by without seeking His forgiveness and power. If you do know Jesus, then walk worthy of your position in Him. **Isai 53:6 All we like sheep have gone astray; we have turned everyone to his own way; and** the LORD hath laid on him the iniquity of us all. 7 He was oppressed, and he was afflicted, yet he opened not his mouth: he is brought as a lamb to the slaughter, and as a sheep before her shearers is dumb, so he openeth not his mouth. 8 He was taken from prison and from judgment: and who shall declare his generation? for he was cut off out of the land of the living: for the transgression of my people was he stricken. 9 And he made his grave with the wicked, and with the rich in his death; because he had done no violence, neither [was any] deceit in his mouth. 11 He shall see of the travail of his soul, [and] shall be satisfied: by his knowledge shall my righteous servant justify many; for he shall bear their iniquities.

"Jesus, thank you for arresting my life, and for coming to me when I wasn't looking. Thank you for giving me a wife who loved you enough to love me when I wasn't lovely. Grant me the strength to give acceptance to the unacceptable and love to the unlovely. Jesus, I love you!"

Murl

A Letter from Ruth, to You

Dear Reader,

Marriage is ordained by God to join two entirely different persons together as one unit. He never promised it would be easy or without problems. I have found that if you honor your vows of "For better or for worse, for richer or for poorer, in sickness and in health; till death do us part," you will discover a true treasure in your mate. Too many people give up and discard their mates like an old shoe at the first source of contention. They spend too much time finding fault and hating instead of perfecting the love that they can give.

Murl and I have been married for thirty-three years. The first couple of months were great, but everything went downhill fast. He wasn't happy with any of his jobs, started drinking heavily, lost his temper at the slightest thing, and I wondered what in the world happened to the happy, charming man I had fallen so madly in love with.

There were many, many times I wanted to run away and live by myself, but there were two things that kept me by his side. The first was my promise to Murl before God that I would stay with him till death, and the second was something my mother told me before our wedding day. She said that now that I had made my "choice" I could never come home by myself if we were having problems. I was to stay and work it out. Thank you, God, for a wise and loving mother!

I tried very hard to keep an outer façade that everything in our marriage was just fine. I didn't confide in any one but God-day in and day out crying for help to make this marriage work. Sometimes our relationship would be good for weeks and weeks and I would think the suffering was finally over. Then something would happen to Murl's self-esteem and I would bear the brunt of his unhappiness again. He never hit me; it was living with his temper, drinking and unfaithfulness. It was not my idea of how my marriage should be.

God got my attention one night in Germany. I had been reading my Bible and at the same time hoping Murl would get hurt or killed while out playing military games. All of a sudden I was paying complete attention to what I was reading. 1 John 2:9-11 states that anyone who claims to be in the light but hates his brother is still in the darkness and the darkness has blinded him. Then I was looking up cross-references and found that anyone who says he loves God and hates his brother is a liar. There are no liars in heaven. If we won't forgive others, then God can't forgive us.

Then God spoke to me out loud. I have heard His voice before and knew who was talking to me. He told me that Murl, even though he had been unfaithful and had done a lot of other things, was forgiven.

Because I refused to forgive Murl and had thought of hurting or killing him, my sins were not forgiven and I was in danger of losing my salvation. I needed to forgive Murl and ask him to forgive me for lying to him about loving him. At that point I did not love him but told him every day that I did.

I wasn't very happy about that and argued with God a little, but I was not going to lose my salvation. It wasn't easy confessing to Murl - he had to drag it out of me - but God is faithful and that was the beginning of a new marriage for us, one that flows more like God intended it to.

It still took several months of crying out to God for help in loving and trusting Murl again. Love is not something you can fall in or out of.

I am so glad I chose to love Murl and stay with him. I believe we were ordained to be together, as God protected me from living as a quadriplegic after a car accident one night during my high school years. He protected me because I had a divine appointment to meet Murl. My neck was broken and I was paralyzed for two weeks until God intervened. While waiting for the ambulance to arrive, Jesus came to me and told me that I would be all right. He told me to just pray and speak to Him as He waited beside the car. I could see His face and feel His presence - it calmed my fears and gave me peace. I now know that if I had been paralyzed I would have never met Murl.

No one can go back and make a brand new start, but you can start from now and make a brand new ending. Don't camp out on the disappointments of life. Move on - God has something better to give you!

Ruth

_____*_____

**"You can start from now
and
make a brand new ending!"**

_____*_____